SIXTY YEARS OF
SAILING FROM THE AGE OF GATSBY TO THE GRENADINE ISLANDS

MW00387768

MEMOIRS OF J. LINTON RIGG

Written by Art Ross

ALL RIGHTS RESERVED: No part of this Book or eBook may be reproduced or transmitted for resale or use by any party other than the individual purchaser who is the sole authorized user of this information. Purchaser is authorized to use any of the information in this publication for his or her own use only. All other reproductions (transmissions or by any means, electronic or mechanical, including photocopying, recording or by any informational storage or retrieval system) is prohibited without express written permission from the publisher, author and copyright holder.

LEGAL NOTICES: While all efforts have not been made to provide effective, verifiable information in this eBook, neither the author nor publisher nor copyright holder assumes any responsibility for errors, inaccuracies or omissions, including any slights of people or organizations, which are unintentional. If advice concerning tax, legal, compliance or related matters is needed, the services of a qualified professional should be sought. This book or eBook is not a source of legal, regulatory compliance, or accounting information, and it should not be regarded as such. This publication is designed to provide accurate and authoritative information in regard to the subject matter covered. It is sold with the understanding that the publisher is not engaged in rendering legal, accounting or other professional service. If legal advice or other expert assistance is required, the services of a competent professional person should be sought. Due to the nature of direct response marketing and varying rules regulating business activities in many fields, some practices proposed in this book or eBook may be deemed unlawful in certain circumstances and locations. Since federal and local laws differ widely, as do codes of conduct for members of professional organizations and agencies, licensee must accept full responsibility for determining the legality and/or ethical character of any and all business transactions and/or practices adopted and enacted in his or her particular field and geographic location, whether or not those transactions and/or practices are suggested, either directly or in-directly, in this Book or eBook. As with any business advice, the reader is strongly encouraged to seek professional counsel before taking action.

NOTE: No guarantees of income or profits are intended by this book or eBook. Many variables affect each individual's results and so your results will vary from the examples given. SP&SK Enterprises, LLC cannot and will not promise your financial or personal success and has no control over what you may do or not do with this guide, and therefore cannot accept the responsibility for your results. You are the only one who can initiate the action, in order to reap your own rewards. Any and all references to persons or businesses, whether living or dead, existing or defunct, are purely coincidental.

Published by: SANDSPublishing

Copyright © SP&SK Enterprises, LLC

First printed March 2013, Edition 1
Revision printed October 2013 Edition 2 (with captions)
ISBN-13:978-1482732559

ISBN-10:1482732556

CREATED & PRINTED IN THE UNITED STATES OF AMERICA, DISTRIBUTED WORLDWIDE.

In Memory of J. Linton Rigg
A True Sailor

INDEX

J. Linton Rigg, the founder of the Carriacou Regatta, was born in Jamaica in 1895. He was raised on the east coast of the United States of America, learned to sail on the Delaware River and the Chesapeake Bay, and prospered in yacht brokering in New York City after completing a marine engineering program at Drexel Institute in Philadelphia, as it was called at the time.

He sailed and played hard in the Gatsby Age, along the way writing cruising guides to the Bahamas and to the Antilles. He was instrumental in starting the National Family Island Regatta in the Bahamas in 1954.

Tyrrel Bay, on the tiny island of Carriacou, is where the story began for me. The following events that occurred there inspired me to assemble this autobiography of Linton, as he was called, using his own words and information from those who knew him.

The country of Grenada is an unlikely target for hurricanes – at least it had been up until 2004 when Ivan landed a direct hit. Carriacou, just north of Grenada, was mostly spared that time. But the following July, Hurricane Emily hit with 90 mph winds, causing heavy damage.

I arrived the next day, by ferry from Grenada. My purpose was to crew with an old friend who had unexpectedly lost her husband the previous year to rum and too little exercise, a cruiser's curse greater than any hurricane. A local van dropped me off at the village of Harvey Vale on the shore of Tyrrel Bay. There was extensive evidence of Emily's visit. I picked my way along the road, navigating over telephone poles and their wires, which were now tangled into the seashore mess left by the storm. My friend picked me up in her dinghy and we managed to get on board her boat, *Phantom*. In the rocking sea left after the storm, the Island Packet 29 lurched up and down, head to tail, like a bucking horse.

The next morning we listened to the VHF radio

FORWARD: BY ART ROSS

net. A call for assistance came from the mangroves. Just north of the harbor these wonderful trees grasp the sand in a way that holds them in place and builds a shelter that had saved so many of the boats and their crew from the storm. The request came from the skipper of *Mermaid of Carriacou*. She had no motor; he could not retrieve her anchor, steer, and haul up the canvas alone. *Phantom* had relied on friends to help her during the storm and she was anxious to return the favor, especially having me aboard as another hand, so off we went.

As we approached *Mermaid* I realized that this wasn't just any boat, but a locally-built wooden vessel, much different than I was used to. We came astern, and the skipper yelled that one of us had to steer as he raised the anchor.

I jumped up on the transom to see the deck of an old and beautiful boat, along with an anxious and irritated owner. "Take the wheel," he said, and, "Where did you come from, who are you, and do you like American politics?" all in one breath.

As I became familiar with the helm, he was making me dizzy with constant and out-of-context questions. We got underway, our little inflatable pulling the heavy boat; only in the lee of the mangroves would this be possible. As we came around a bend, we passed by a creek – the creek that once inspired a young boy years ago to dream a remarkable vision. But I had no idea of this dream or boy as I steered clear out of the mangroves into the bay and was told by the owner to "get off now." *Mermaid's* owner is John Smith, an icon owning an iconic boat. Living aboard a traditional boat, with nothing traditional about himself, he was certainly a different kind of character.

Back in the dinghy, we made our way through the anchorage to *Phantom*, and that was that – just another moment in the strange days that were to follow. I knew that this was not going to be the usual few weeks in the islands that I have come to love

Linton's home Tranquillity in Windward, Carriacou

during my winter visits from Pennsylvania. I would later find out from another icon of Carriacou, the artist Canute Caliste, that he and Linton were linked by "the mermaid." As a child, Canute Caliste had a vision of a mermaid at the creek we passed near the opening to the mangroves. Linton arrived here in the 1960s at the peak of both of their lives. Canute was a famous painter, musician and boatbuilder; Rigg was a sailor extraordinaire and in need of a home, a boat, and a purpose.

They found each other, and here the end of my story begins.

The fortieth anniversary of the Carriacou Regatta was happening while I was there.

Because of his love of competitive sailing, Linton developed this event, just as he had started the Bahamas regatta years before. A part of the festivities was a special dinner party at what had been Linton's home on the northeastern part of the island in the boat-building town of Windward,

facing the islands of Petite Martinique and Petit St. Vincent. He named his home Tranquillity. The current owner, and our hostess, was Eutha McLaren, daughter of Zepherine McLaren who built *Mermaid* for the first Carriacou Regatta. Rigg had partnered with McLaren, buying the materials while McLaren did the carpentry. The boat was named after Canute Caliste's vision.

I was having fun; local music played as we drank rum and ate barracuda stew. The home was inviting, and I strolled into the living area; there I met Eutha.

She offered me a tour and I gladly accepted. We went from room to room, ending up in Linton's bedroom, just as he had left it forty years ago. Logbooks and world-band radio caught my eye. I was enthralled. As we got back to the living room there was a guest book that she asked me to sign. I wrote "Captain Art Ross, New Hope, PA." I thanked her for such an extraordinary tour of Linton Rigg's home, and went back outside to tell my friends

Tranqillity's living room

8

excitedly of my experience.

Moments later I was approached by a lady who, by her looks, was not local. She asked if I was Captain Art, and when I said that I was, she said she was Betty Anne Rigg of Doylestown, Pennsylvania, the next town west of my home. She was the honored guest of the evening, along with her husband, John Rigg, the son of Bunny, Linton's younger brother. I was astonished, and we spent the rest of the evening playing "one degree of separation" and promising to stay in touch.

We met back in Pennsylvania a few weeks later for a casual dinner. I gave them pictures that I took of the island event, and they gave me an unpublished autobiography of parts of John Linton Rigg's life.

I felt I was steering by stars in motion. In Carriacou I had sailed on Linton Rigg's boat, if only for a few hundred yards at the helm, met his family, become instant friends with *Mermaid's* builder and family, and had even seen the creek where Caliste's vision of the mermaid appeared, having had him tell me the story himself – all in a span of forty-eight hours. And now, back home, his words were in my hands.

Captain Art Ross
New Hope
03.20.2013

Eutha McLaren, *Mermaid's* builder Zepherine McLaren's daughter

TO MY SHIPMATES

You who tried on earth to set your mark,
To kindle beacons where it's ways were dark,
To whom for the world who had no need of you,
It once had seemed a little thing, to die.
Sad Comrade, we were shipmates in one crew,
Somewhere we sailed together, you and I.

You, against whom all fates have been arrayed,
Who heard the voice of God, and disobeyed,
Who reckless, and with all your battles lost,
Went forth again another chance to try.
Oh we have been on the same rough ocean tossed,
And watched the stars together, you and I.

Sad comrade, if at last, your ship should find
Home, and all the sheltered heavens left behind,
I shall be with you in that merry crew,
Under the same old flag we used to fly.
But if, at last, of every promise shorn,
With leaking timbers and with canvas torn,
Still for the pride of seamanship sail you,
There also, in your chartless ship sail I.

A poem found in Linton's logbook in his home.
Author Sidney Royse Lysaght (1860 - 1941)

overleaf photo:
Mangrove anchorage in Carriacou

With the passage of time, as in a long sea voyage, memories are apt to converge into a tapestry of mosaic images. So it is with my recollections of Carriacou in 1967-68. Some features of my time there appear to me with pin-point clarity. Others are blurred around the edges and a few are dark and featureless, swirling into a virtual black hole. I find that taking time, now and again, to write down my memories and flesh out details can be a cathartic experience.

In September 1967 I arrived in Carriacou, to teach at Bishop's College. The town of Hillsborough was, largely, made up of Front Street, Back Street and Paterson Street. The town had one guest house and one hotel of note: the Mermaid Tavern.

I soon discovered that the Mermaid Tavern was owned by an enigmatic individual by the name of J. Linton Rigg. I quickly came to hear the tales of Linton's seafaring adventures. He stood tall in the community and was held in reverence and respect.

Having said that, the Mermaid Tavern was a tourist destination, so not a place I frequented too often. Linton remained, therefore, a somewhat distant figure – someone I nodded to on the street or greeted as he stood by the front door of the tavern. However, Carriacou was where Linton spent his latter years and it seems apposite, at this point, to give a flavour of the island and the people with whom he shared his remaining years.

At the end of a teaching day my destinations of choice were the sea, the beach, the sports field for football or cricket, the principal's home in Back Street or Lord Joseph's rum shop. This small, wooden building that was Lord Joseph's, stood (and still stands, as far as I know) just opposite the main entrance to the old site of Bishop's College on Front Street and a few doors along from the Mermaid Tavern.

Lord, that was his birth name, was a devoted anglophile. A picture of a young queen and duke

photo opposite:
Author's photo of *Mermaid* underway

INTRODUCTION: BY BILL CAMERON

decorated the wall of his small back room. A bare table and a few chairs were where we "fired our jack," took a "Carib," played domino, and debated matters political. Being the sole Englishman in the group I was chosen as Commonwealth representative and made to "take the chair" in debates. In this way we passed many joyous hours, clattering domino and discussing island independence and Commonwealth affairs.

Any dissent and Lord would show his disapproval by pulling himself up to full height, put a finger to his lips and make a low, guttural cough – twice. The cough would then morph into a rumbling belly laugh as he poured out a jack for everyone to toast the queen. One must remember these were days before the dreaded "box" had made its appearance on the island. Entertainment was made on the hoof. Discussion, debate, and social interaction were at the heart of this vibrant community.

Cricket, football, swimming, diving, dancing, dominoes, fetes, Big Drum, and sailing were all part of the social scene. Weddings, funerals, maroon, saracas and wakes all formed part of a daily and seasonal round, shared by villages and communities scattered around Carriacou and Petite Martinique. In addition, of course, we had carnival, boat launching ceremonies, and the annual regatta.

Linton is famous for kick starting boat building on the island in the '60s when he had his famous sloop, *Mermaid of Carriacou* designed and built. He then offered a substantial reward to anyone who could build another with enough speed and sail power to beat her. The Carriacou Regatta was born in 1964 and *Mermaid* won her class in many regattas thereafter. This is now the stuff of legend. Into the mix we must add boat builder Zepherine McLaren and the community of Windward, which lay at the centre of beach boat building in Carriacou.

Let us imagine we are hitching a lift on one of the richly painted, open sided-buses from

Playing dominoes in a rum shack in Carriacou

Hillsborough market to Windward. We climb the open steps and join the Kayaks on board to participate in a fun-packed ride, consisting of merry chatter, clucking chickens, vegetable boxes and loud greetings to passing pedestrians.

The Commer engine rattles and whines as we descend from Dover down the twisting road into Windward village. Neat, red- and grey-roofed gingerbread houses line the street into the village. They stand perched on concrete pillars. Steps lead up to a narrow balcony and a welcoming front door. Lace curtains flap in the open windows. Pipes and guttering, arranged at crazy angles, lead down into concrete water cisterns, so necessary during the long, dry season.

The bus draws up opposite the jetty. Men crash dominoes on to the table outside the rum shop, dogs wander the street looking for scraps, conch shells and flotsam lie scattered on the beach. Further up the beach, amongst the swaying palms, standing on chocks, are the keel and ribs of a sloop under construction. Small children run playfully around her stern.

From the shade of the palms raise your eyes and look out to sea. Lift your gaze beyond the wooden jetty and past the merchant sloops riding at anchor in the blue calm of Watering Bay. In the middle distance waves break over the fringing reef that trails down towards Grand Bay. Rising green out of the azure waters, you see the conical hill of Petite Martinique flanked by Petit St. Vincent to the north and Petit Dominique to the south. Turn your gaze north and be astonished at the string of island pearls that are the Tobago Keys.

In 1968 this was a scene that had remained largely unchanged for a hundred years. Enoe, McLaren, McLawrence, Steill, Compton and Roberts – these families had built boats, worked the land, and sailed and traded the length of the Caribbean islands for generations. Just south of the

photo right:
Zepherine McLaren, on right, passed away December 29, 2009. His knowledge and expertise in boat building cannot be replaced easily. His vessels like *Mermaid of Carriacou* still sail, and on its hatch is a plaque-mounted saying: "God does not deduct from the alloted life span the time spent sailing."

village was Tranquillity, the abode of J. Linton Rigg. This was a larger, more impressive house, built in the Colonial style. On his front garden the sails for *Mermaid* were laid out to be stitched and repaired. This was where Linton relaxed, reminisced, and made his plans "to liven up de island culture" with a legendary boat and a regatta that has "sailed an unstoppable course" into the twenty-first century.

Now, as we roll back the years, we remember the vignettes and telescoped memories of an island life which is slowly changing and being dragged into the modern world. But hey, the Kayaks are still the same friendly, buoyant people they always were. They're still taking pride in the sloops, fishing boats and speedboats that are being constructed on the beaches of Carriacou and PM. I imagine the ghosts of all those old timers still linger on the beach doin' "fete as bush." There's ole Linton and Zepherine makin' "pappy show," "firing one" and laughing at the "simi dimi" everyone making of them. But don't take my word for it ...

"Come you coming, you go see."

Bill Cameron
Lyme Regis
18.04.2012

Glossary of Dialect and Slang Terms

Fete as bush - A grand party with lots to eat and drink
Pappy show - Mock and make fun of each other
Fire one - Take (knock back) a drink (of jack iron)
Simi dimi - Exaggerated fuss
Come you coming, you go see - Come and you'll soon find out for yourself
Jack Iron - Extra strength rum

(With thanks to Christine David from *Folklore of Carriacou* for the dialect and slang translations.)

Art would like to thank Bill Cameron for his introduction and explaining some of what he experienced in the sixties in Carriacou"; for more about Bill: http://www.carriacou1968.com/

photo opposite:
Bahama Moorings © CarolRossPhotography.com

The sea is in my blood, as it must have been in the blood of my ancestors, who sailed from England to the West Indies in 1795.

The lure of the sea is like that of a moth to the flame, an irresistible craving to be near to it, on it or be in it. To be on a ship on the sea is a supreme satisfaction. Next to that is to be on an island surrounded by the sea.

For these, and other personal reasons, I have journeyed through an interesting life in many countries towards a permanent mooring on Carriacou, one of the most beautiful islands in the West Indies and even in the world. A few of my little adventures along this journey are herewith described.

photo opposite:
Linton at the helm

MEMOIRS FORWARD: BY J. LINTON RIGG

The beginning of my yachting career, or at least my first experience with boats, was one which I do not remember very well. As a matter of fact, I hardly remember it at all, though, my dear mother often told me about it in great detail and also with evident enjoyment and laughter. In fact, when I became fairly prominent in the yachting world, my mother used to tease me about this first experience of mine as a yachtsman.

My family were then living in Jamaica where I was born. Our house was high up in the mountains in Jamaica and from the house the sea could be seen at a distance. I often gazed at it with fascination and wonder, never dreaming that some day I would sail for thousands of miles over it, even in my own boat, too. The only water nearby on which a boat or even a toy boat could be sailed was a duck pond, which was some distance away from the house.

On the appointed day, the governor of Jamaica, a very august and important gentleman, was coming to take tea with my father and mother at our house in the mountains. At the appointed time the governor arrived promptly as usual, all trigged out in a very elegant full-dress uniform topped off by a most elegant pith helmet, which had a spike on the top of it. His reason for wearing all this gear was that he had been attending a very important ceremony nearby. As was usual on occasions of this sort, tea was a very elaborate affair, actually a high tea that lasted an hour or two. When the governor was finally ready to leave, his pith helmet could not be found. A search was inaugurated all over the house; no sign of the pith helmet. The search was then extended to the grounds around the house with still no signs of the pith helmet. Also, my mother happened to notice that there was no sign of little Linton.

With a sinking heart, she began to connect little Linton with the pith helmet and the duck pond. Well, when the search party finally arrived at the duck pond, there they found little Linton with the

photo opposite:
Linton's early days at sea

CHAPTER 1: MY FIRST BOAT

pith helmet, which he had rigged up as a boat. The craft, if you might call it that, was now rigged as a cat boat with a stick sticking up in the middle of it and a sheet of paper from a copy book on the stick to make a sail, and, of course, the keel was the spike that steadied her. Little Linton was sailing her up and down the duck pond, much to his delight. The governor was not amused; neither was my father, although my mother said she could hardly keep her face straight. The governor's farewell was rather cool. Then, of course, I had to face my father, who proceeded to give me a small lecture followed by a thorough good hiding. This was no patty-pat affair but a first-class, pants-down licking with a strap. The idea that such a licking breeds resentment in a child towards a parent is simply nonsense, for I adored my father and never held it against him at any time. Mother said that after the licking, in tears and between sobs, I kept saying, "Oh, but mother it was such a perfect boat with a keel and everything." So that was, you might say, my first boat and first experience with yachting, and I was only four years old at the time.

CARPE DIEM

Mah day is today!
You kin have, I say,
Tomorrow — which ain' come,
Yestiddy—which done gone—
Take 'em bofe, I say,
But—gimme today!

Today is mah fren',
Today is de day foh me!
Yestiddy I borrow,
Got to pay tomorrow,
But today—I spen',
Today is mah fren'!

Trouble come today?
I say, "Back away!
Git out, ole man Sorrow!
Call roun' tomorrow!
Ain't you hear me say
Dat today's mah day!"

Carpe Diem found amongst Linton's photos

photo opposite:
Rigg boys on Delaware Bay

However, about eight years later, I was to make a really long-wished-for trip, and it turned out to be a very disastrous one for me.

My father, who was the youngest son of a large family, had gone into the Church, much to the amusement of his sporting brothers. His ancestors and mine had come out from England in 1795 and built up a small fortune in bananas and sugar. Most of it had been lost in depressed markets, hurricanes and other calamities, not the least of which was the crooked and unscrupulous lawyer who misappropriated many of the funds left to the children. The estate at Retreat near Ocho Rios, Jamaica, was the principal plantation and it was surrounded by three others, all owned by my grandfather. Most of the natives in that area are descended from the slaves he owned.

Although human slavery was a deplorable thing, and undoubtedly there were some plantations where the slaves were treated in a beastly way, there were others on which the slaves were treated more as valuable servants than as slaves. Such a place was Retreat plantation. I remember my grandfather telling me that when the slaves were emancipated and given their freedom by the British Government, the slaves at Retreat came crying to him, "We don't want to go nowhere but here, for who would look after us." Most of them never left the district.

Many of my ancestors are buried in the church in Retreat and in the churchyard; my grandfather built the church and presented it to the community as a gift.

My father was a big man, over six feet, and like many an old-fashioned English country parson, a great sportsman and athlete. He played cricket, tennis, golf, football, was a good shot, a strong swimmer and a superb horseman. One of his passions also was fishing and for that, he usually went to Canada for salmon fishing. It was also his belief that any white man who lived in the tropics

photo opposite:
Rigg family in Easton MD, Linton far right

CHAPTER 2: MY FATHER

should spend at least one month in northern waters or northern climates every year, and always keep in good health. It was on one of his trips to Canada that he met and became friendly with another ardent fisherman, Bishop Rhinelander, who happened to be the Bishop of Pennsylvania, USA. Bishop Rhinelander invited my father to come to Philadelphia to visit him, which my father did. He was very happily received, and among the people whom he met, was one of the leading members of the du Pont family of Wilmington, Delaware. I think it was Mr. Coleman du Pont and he persuaded my father to come down to Delaware for a visit.

While he was there, they showed him a beautiful old church, Immanuel Church in New Castle, Delaware, one of the oldest churches in America. My father fell in love with it, and when it was offered to him he readily accepted. He never even bothered to come back to Jamaica; he simply wrote to my mother and told her to sell all the property, the cattle, carriages, and all the things we owned and discharge the servants. Bringing only two servants with her, she and the children were to come to America. My poor dear mother had to take care of all those things and eventually we started off from Jamaica on a little United Fruit Company vessel called the *Annotto* or *Annetto*, I can't remember which, in October of 1907.

Thomas Coleman du Pont (December 11, 1863 – November 11, 1930)
An American engineer and politician. He was president of E.I. du Pont Nemours and Company, eventually owning the company with his two cousins. He also served parts of two United States Senate terms. Source: Wikipedia

photo overleaf:
Local boats in mangroves in Carriacou

photo opposite:
Father, Rev. John Rigg

NEW DEAN FOR EASTON

EASTON, MD.—The Rev. John Rigg, rector of St. Thomas' Parish, Diocese of Washington, has been chosen dean of Trinity Cathedral, Easton, and takes up his new work June 1st. He will also direct the rural work in the vicinity of the see city.

The Rev. Mr. Rigg is a native of Jamaica, and was ordained to the priesthood by Archbishop Nuttall in 1893. Previous to this, he had taken his degree in arts from Durham University, England, and had prepared for orders at the Jamaica Church Theological College. In 1907 he came to the United States to take up work in Newcastle, Del., and he went to Riverton, N. J., in 1912. The Philadelphia Divinity School awarded him the degree of Bachelor of Divinity the year before.

In 1921 Mr. Rigg accepted the historic and important rural parish of Croom, Md., for a long time the residence of Bishop Claggett, the first Bishop of Maryland, and his burial place until the translation of his body to Washington Cathedral. There he built up the Church among the country people so that now the chief service each Sunday is a celebration of the Holy Eucharist. He is also deeply interested in the Society of the Nazarene, and has been quite prominent in the ministry of this society in the Diocese of Washington.

Mr. Rigg is a priest of striking personality to whom men in particular are quickly drawn. Advices state that he has

It started out as a fairly pleasant trip, but when we were off the Carolina coast we were caught in the tail end of an autumn hurricane, and that is something I did remember and will never forget. There was such a tremendous sea that the little *Annotto* was hove-to for over twelve hours and I think everybody on board was seasick, certainly including mother and her five little children. She used to amuse me by telling me that I went to the captain and offered him one million dollars, or one million pounds, I forget which, if he would only stop the ship for a few hours so that we could all have a little rest. At any rate we survived that and arrived in Philadelphia in the middle of a snow storm with only tropical clothing on. I will never forget that either. Mother brought from Jamaica with us only two servants, both very pretty colored girls and no sooner had we arrived in New Castle, Delaware than all the colored men around there started to pay attention to these girls. They were quite fascinated by them. At any rate, within the next two or three months they both became pregnant. Both left and went their various ways, and we never saw them again. My poor mother then found herself without any servants at all.

She had never done a lick of work in her life; now she had to learn to cook, wash, and do all the other things besides looking after five children with a sixth on the way. The sixth was my brother, Bunny, who was born at the rectory in New Castle, Delaware and who has today become one of the leading ocean racing men in the world, a fine sailor man.

New Castle, Delaware is a very quaint and charming little riverside town and used to be the principal seaport of Delaware. The great Delaware River was only two miles wide at this point, and a great deal of ocean shipping passes up and down it. As the river is fresh water, a tremendous amount of ice comes down in the winter time, and at New Castle a safe anchorage was made many years ago

photo opposite:
Children in Delaware, Linton on right

CHAPTER 3: TO AMERICA

by erecting several stone and concrete islands set in the river offshore. These act as ice breakers. Inside these in the winter time there is usually a fleet of small vessels: fishermen from the banks, working boats of various sorts, and the occasional square-rigger. Every day in the winter, when all the other boys would be playing games or skating (I never could learn how to skate properly), I would be down there on those ships listening to stories of the sea, picking up nautical lore, learning to splice, to tie knots, even the proper seaman's language. To a small boy it was paradise enough. I was never happy at school for many reasons. To begin with, my hearing had been impaired by an early attack of scarlet fever while I was at school in Jamaica. For fifty years I suffered that handicap until in 1962 when an operation by the celebrated Dr. Silcox in Philadelphia restored my hearing to normal. For many years I had to wear a hearing aid. Then, too, with my English accent which I never quite lost, I was always ridiculed by my Yankee schoolmates, which involved me in many a bloody fight.

The men on those ships in the harbor were men of many different nationalities and broader horizons and experience, so they did not mind all these little things which so much annoyed my fellow schoolmates. I felt more at home with these men on the ships and spent most of my time with them.

photo opposite:
'Hat's Off', Linton in his early years

Then in the spring, when the ships were gone, came the great shad fishing industry into which I entered with enthusiasm. In those days shad came up the river in large schools and were caught in enormous gill nets laid out across the river. Some of those nets were half a mile long and some of them even longer than that. The shad boats were long, open boats about twenty feet in length with a lot of beam. They were handled entirely by oars. To lay out and haul those nets was man's work and rowing the boat in the river chop was no cinch either. I did both and it gave me solid muscle, which saved my life more than once.

The shad fishing industry in New Castle was really quite fantastic in those days, for one whole trainload of shad was shipped out of New Castle every day during the shad season. My small share of profits, due to my help with the work, was enough to enable me to buy the materials with which to build myself a boat. I just had to have a boat of my own, my very own, so I proceeded to build one. I built her in the attic in the rectory and knowing nothing about ship building, my first boat was an awful failure. She was only a twelve footer but with so much beam that when she was finished I found that I could not get her out of the attic at the rectory. I had to unbuild her to take her outside and then rebuild her. She was never much of a success. She leaked like a sieve and my father was afraid that I would drown myself in her. Eventually he said that if I would consent to break her up, he would buy me a real boat. For quite a long while I had had my eye on a lovely little double-ender, a rowing boat, owned by an old Norwegian called Gus. He and I had become quite friendly, and he had allowed me to use her occasionally. I told my father about that and father then persuaded old Gus to sell the boat to me.

I think the deal involved about fifteen dollars in cash, an old suit of clothes, and a box of cigars. At any rate, Gus' little double-ender became mine. He

photo opposite:
Young sailors, Linton and Bunny

CHAPTER 4: IN THE ATTIC

was an experienced Norwegian builder and she was a lovely boat with very narrow planks. He had, in addition to building a very tight hull, strapped her all around with bronze straps or brass straps so that she was almost indestructible. She was a wonderful little boat, my second boat, and I named her *Coquette*.

Rev. Rigg and the church choir in Delaware

photo opposite:
Linton at the helm on the Delaware River

On the *Coquette* I cruised all the way from New Castle to the Delaware capes, rowing all the way. The trip down was uneventful but in the middle of the Delaware Bay, which is a very nasty piece of water with heavy currents, a terrific line squall came roaring up, making a nasty sea. I was getting a little bit desperate because the ebb tide was sweeping me out to the open sea. I saw a big schooner anchored some distance away, and after a hard pull I came up alongside her and jumped up on deck with the painter of the *Coquette* in my hand. She was a big Gloucester fisherman and the crew were all down below eating. When they looked up and saw me in the companionway they yelled, "My God boy, where in hell did you come from?" and then they remembered me from having come aboard the schooner the previous winter at New Castle, so they were my friends. They took my *Coquette* on board, lashed her down comfortably, and took me off to the banks with them for a nice comfortable cruise and brought me back to New Castle in about a week, at least as I remembered it, probably about two weeks. At any rate, I always remember two things about those Gloucester fishermen. First was how well they fed, both in quantity and quality, and secondly, how very quietly they worked their ships: no shouting orders, no confusion, every man knows his job and does it as quietly and efficiently as possible. The captain hardly ever raised his voice and most of his orders were just hand signals. Real professionals, those men.

photo opposite:
Wishing for wind on Delaware Bay

CHAPTER 5: COQUETTE

Alas, the day came when we were to leave New Castle. My father's popularity as a parish priest had spread and he was now called to the Episcopal Church in Riverton, New Jersey, a call which he accepted because he considered that a better climate for the education of his children. It did enable me to study engineering at the Drexel Institute in Philadelphia.

Now a parson's family has to become accustomed to moving around from place to place, never having a real home of their own. Every move, of course, had a certain element of excitement about it. While I was very sad about leaving all my sailormen and fishermen friends in New Castle, the news that, in Riverton, there was a yacht club proved more exciting. Working boats are very sturdy and interesting and nice, but yachts are the thoroughbreds of the sea. Every sailor, I think, dreams of someday having a pretty little boat used only for pleasure, which in fact is a yacht. So we moved to Riverton, New Jersey, a small town on the Delaware River above Philadelphia, and I became the secretary of the Riverton Yacht Club and, therefore, a genuine yachtsman at last.

Riverton is typical of a small, pretentious American suburban town, with its semi-sophistication, narrow-mindedness, middle-class morality and petty jealousies. I hated the place, but I loved the river. In my years there I learned a great deal about the winds, the use of currents, and the proper handling of small boats.

One of my first activities as secretary of the Riverton Yacht Club was to organize and promote the formation of a one-design class for racing. All my pocket money had been spent on buying yachting magazines, particularly the *Rudder,* whose editor, Thomas Fleming Day, corresponded religiously with me, becoming my friend and mentor.

His writings convinced me that only a truly one-

Thomas Fleming Day (1861 - August 19, 1927)
A sailboat designer and sailboat racer. He was the founding editor of Rudder, a monthly magazine about boats. He was the first to win the annual New York to Bermuda race.
Source: Wikipedia

photo opposite:
Linton and Bunny racing on the Delaware River

CHAPTER 6: RIVERTON

design class was the answer to young, impoverished yachtsmen who wanted some real racing. A retired naval architect, an Englishman named Mr. Hill, living in Riverton, became interested and contributed free of charge a set of plans for a nice sixteen-foot sloop, something like a modern Lightning in design but with a typical English sliding Gunter rig. They were to be of the simplest construction and cost about $150 each without sails. About twelve were built and we drew numbers for them. Mine was number eleven and I named her *Little Haste,* remembering the old adage, "more haste, less speed," so conversely less haste, more speed. With my small brothers as crew, we won thirty-six races in *Little Haste* and we were never beaten. Looking back at it, there was very little to be proud of in that the competition was negligible – a lot of weekend pleasure sailors who took little interest in their boats between races while we, on the other hand, worked on our boat just as if she were a candidate for the America's Cup.

Before every race we hauled her out, scrubbed her off, and sanded the bottom with the finest sandpaper. When that was dry we varnished it, and over the wet varnish we sprinkled powdered graphite. When that was set, we got all the boys and their friends to polish it with newspaper till the bottom was like glass. The sails we kept in a dry room in the rectory, and we frequently recut and resewed them ourselves to preserve their perfect shape – that's how we won races.

By the time I was eighteen years old I had made up my mind that I wanted to spend the rest of my life with boats, and the best way to achieve that was to become a naval architect. My father agreed and advised me to talk the matter over with his cousin, Ernest Rigg, who in his own right was a very distinguished naval architect.

Cousin Ernest was chief naval architect of the New York Shipbuilding Company of Camden, New

Man's best friend, Rigg family dog

Jersey, and was engaged in designing and building warships, battle cruisers, aircraft carriers, and all other such vessels for the United States Navy. He encouraged the idea of my becoming an architect, but warned me that the proper course, which he and all other qualified architects had been through in Scotland, required four years in college learning the theory of it all and three alternate years working in a shipyard learning the practice of the theories – seven years in all. He offered to start me off in the New York Shipbuilding Company.

So one particularly hot and humid summer, instead of sailing my boat on the cool river, I went to work in the yard of the New York Shipbuilding Company in Camden, New Jersey, and was started off as a painter. Every morning, already dripping with perspiration in the heat, I was given a bucket of red lead and a brush, let down into the bowels of some battleship or aircraft carrier and was put to work painting naked steelwork. Usually all around me was the nerve-shattering shriek of riveting hammers, the roaring of electric tools and other noises that sounded like bedlam. This kept up all day long except for the lunch hour. After eight hours of breathing in the fumes of fresh paint in a closed space, we, the painters, would emerge completely deaf from the noise and covered with red lead from head to foot. I stood it for four months. Then I decided that I simply did not wish to be that kind of naval architect.

My next job was with the Bell Telephone Company tracing and measuring electrolysis in underground electric cables, a subject which I had studied and was familiar with. It was a little better than the ship yard painting job, but not much because it required me to go crawling up and down manholes all over the streets of Philadelphia. As I always liked to arrive at work clean and well dressed, I usually went home looking like a tramp. By that time my spirits were very low.

Mother at the table in Easton MD

However, a good friend of mine, Mr. R.A. Hollingshead of Camden, New Jersey, who was a member of the yacht club and head of a large firm where they made soaps and soap articles, had become interested in my acquired knowledge of yachts and the basic principles of naval architecture. He suggested that I ought to become a yacht broker and, if I wished to do so, he would give me the first commission to go and find a yacht suitable for him and buy it for him. That was a great break, and overnight I found myself projected into the very interesting world of yacht and ship brokerage, which I then followed for the next thirty years.

With the proceeds of my first transaction as a yacht broker, I set myself up in business in an office in the Bellevue Court Building in Philadelphia. For the first few weeks I had nothing at all to do except to watch the antics of the occupants in the bedrooms in the Bellevue-Stratford Hotel only a few feet away from my desk. One could usually tell whether they were married or not. The married ones usually pulled down the blinds, the others couldn't wait to do so – it was very enlightening. Soon business started to come in and a gentleman, a member of the Philadelphia Corinthian Yacht Club, came in and listed his yacht with me for sale. He said he was selling her because she had been out-built by the new boats in the twenty-one-foot class, so she had no chance to win races. I went to Essington with him to examine her and fell in love with her at first sight and bought her myself, thus becoming my own first customer. She was a Herreshoff creation, a beautiful thing designed and built by old Captain Nat Herreshoff himself. She was planked with mahogany and bright finished; she was a joy to sail. Her name was *Quakeress*. Being now the possessor of a first-class racing boat, I was very anxious to try my ability against better competition than I could find in Riverton.

Rev. John Rigg

photo opposite:
Mother and family dog

I knew that the Philadelphia Corinthian Yacht Club had some very first-class racing men, notably George and Robert Barry, and their newer and faster boat had consistently beaten the *Quakeress*. Nevertheless, I knew the river, the wind currents, the ties and their eddies, and *Quakeress* was a ghost in light air, so I figured that I had a reasonable chance against them if they would race. I, therefore, forwarded to the Philadelphia Corinthian Yacht Club a formal challenge from the Riverton Yacht Club for a match race between the *Quakeress* and their best twenty-one footer. That was the twenty-one-foot waterline class; the boats themselves were about thirty-two or three feet overall. This challenge was ignored and never even acknowledged. I found out many years later that it was considered quite an impertinence for a little jerkwater yacht club, as they called us, to challenge the ancient and honourable Philadelphia Corinthians.

The new owner of the *Quakeress* was considered to be an upstart, and some of the older mainline members of the Corinthian Yacht Club went so far as to carry their animosity towards me into the business and club circles in New York, even after I moved away from Philadelphia and went to live in New York. Only Sherman Hoyt stood up for me; he always loved and helped the younger generation – a wonderful friend he was. Having failed to get any worthwhile racing competition for the *Quakeress* on the Delaware River, I decided to take her for a cruise.

C. Sherman Hoyt
His memoirs are a fascinating history of sailing since the 1880s and earned him the title of the world's most famous yachtsman of his era. His travels brought him in contact with Adolph Hitler, King George V, William Tecumseh Sherman (his grand uncle), and of course Linton, among others. Sherman had an extraordinary life that took him around the world in adventures and voyages. As an America's Cup enthusiast he served as the New York Yacht Club representative aboard *Shamrock IV* in 1920. His matchless genius at the helm and Harold Vanderbilt's ability to utilize the various talents of his crew to their best effect brought them the cup on *Rainbow*.
Source: Herreshoff Marine Museum

photo opposite:
The boys, right to left, Linton, Bunny and Phil Rigg

CHAPTER 7: CORINTHIANS

49

With my two small brothers as crew, we sailed her up the Delaware River to the entrance of the Delaware and Raritan Canal up near Trenton, New Jersey. We then towed her through the Raritan Canal, then to the Raritan River and sailed down into New York waters. The two young boys then went home to Riverton, and in subsequent stages I managed to sail her all the way to Marblehead, Massachusetts, which was then the mecca for all racing craft.

Among my proud possessions was a small booklet entitled *Yachting Etiquette*. It was edited by my old friend, Thomas Fleming Day, and published by the Rudder Publishing Company, and I knew it by heart. Such a book is badly needed today. I wrote one myself, but my publishers decided that there would be no demand for it, so they did not print it. In this little book, among other things, the yachtsman was advised that whenever visiting the anchorage of another yacht club he should always

pay a courtesy call on the commodore of the yacht club being visited. When paying such a call, he should always go properly dressed. Now having come to anchor off the Eastern Yacht Club in Marblehead Harbor I put on my white trousers, my double-breasted blue jacket, and my yachting cap, all pretty well mildewed but still presentable, and went ashore in the club launch to pay my courtesy call on the commodore. Passing over the lawn up towards the clubhouse I saw an elderly looking man lying down on the grass under a tree. I stopped to speak to him. He wore khaki trousers and an old dark flannel shirt, and I took him to be a gardener. When I asked where I could find the commodore, he said, "What do you want with him?" to which I replied, "I am paying a courtesy call on him; I am a visiting yachtsman." Without a smile or change of expression, he said, "Sit down, son; I am the commodore, my name is Adams." That is how I first met that great yachtsman, treasurer of Harvard

photo opposite:
The boys growing up as sailors

CHAPTER 8: CRUISING AND YACHTING

University, and subsequently, secretary of the Navy, Charles Francis Adams.

He was very interested in my cruise. He asked me a lot of questions about it and invited me to sleep on his "Q" boat the *Ahmeek*, an invitation which I readily accepted as the little cuddy shelter on the *Quakeress* was not quite comfortable in that cold climate.

I next saw Mr. Adams some ten years later. It was in the palace of the king of Spain, King Alfonso, at Santander in Spain. We had both raced across the Atlantic; I on the *Pinta* in the small class, and he on the *Atlantic* in the large class. I walked up to him and said, "Mr. Adams, I don't know if you remember me." His eyes twinkled and he said, "I will never forget you; the boy who pays courtesy calls on commodores."

My life in Philadelphia was very pleasant, comfortable and secure, for I lived with my parents in Riverton, commuting to my office in Philadelphia every day. However, I found it stifling, stifling to my energies and ambitions. Most of the men who I got to know in Philadelphia were successful businessmen – smug, self-satisfied, and seemed to value only one thing, security: To my mind, security is a necessity for women but an unbecoming thing for a man, particularly a young man. It dampens his enthusiasm for life, for adventure, for engaging in anything with an element of danger in it. Ever since my boyhood I had rebelled against conformity and never wanted security. Of course, the hardest part of striking out alone is the breaking of those dear and precious family ties with which one is blessed in childhood. It is a price that one must pay, and it is a big one. I had to pay that price with very high interest later in my life when I went to live on an island in the Bahamas and then again when I settled in Carriacou in the Windward Islands. I seldom see my dear brothers and sisters and some of my best friends, and I do miss them terribly.

Charles Francis Adams III
In 1920, he skippered the America's Cup defender *Resolute* and soon became known as the "Dean of American Helmsmen." He was inducted into the America's Cup Hall of Fame (1993).The Charles Francis Adams Memorial Trophy for yacht racing was established in his memory, and the Navy destroyer USS *Distroyer Charles F Adams,* was dedicated in his honor.
Source: Wikipedia

photo opposite:
Family photo, Linton top left

New York would be exciting but also very expensive. The competition was fierce but the horizon was broader, and one met interesting people from all over the world. So I pulled up my stakes and moved to New York with only one hundred dollars in my pocket. I knew only two people in New York, my friends Thomas Fleming Day and old William P. Stephens, the editor of Lloyd's Register. Mr. Stephens invited me to live with his family until I got going, which I did.

Within a year I had a hundred friends and had probably met a thousand people. That is what happens to you in New York if you are lucky, and I was lucky. If a few people find you interesting, they take the trouble to introduce you to interesting people who put you in touch with other interesting people. Through Thomas Fleming Day I met the famous marine artist, Charles Patterson, who became one of my very best friends and who painted that wonderful picture of my yacht *Filatonga*, which has been admired so much by yachting people. Through him I met Christopher Morley, Don Marquis and others, and attended the lunches of the "three hours for lunch club," where I met many writers and artists. I got to know the wonderful Clara Thomas, who at that time had about the only recognized salon in New York. At her house on Gramercy Square I met more interesting people, many of the theatrical crowd whom I adored, in fact, I kept falling in love with actresses. I sold a large houseboat with a piano in it to Jerome Kern and I heard him play "Smoke Gets in Your Eyes" on it, probably for the first time.

As an amateur boxer, I got to know many of the prize fighting and sporting crowd. I often sparred with some of the leading prize fighters, some really tough ones, too. Old Mr. Stephens took me around with him to all the yachting meets, and I got to know so many yachtsmen that I can hardly remember all their names. I did remember the names of their

photo opposite:
Linton working out

CHAPTER 9: NEW YORK CITY

boats. But probably the most interesting part of that New York life, to me at any rate, was meeting the odd collection of deep-sea yachtsmen who sailed in to New York Harbor and were usually entertained and often honoured by the Cruising Club of America, of which I was then a member.

Rigg and his best friend

photo opposite:
A family sail day on Delaware Bay

One of the most interesting was old Harry Pidgeon and thereby hangs a tale. Harry Pidgeon was a very remarkable man. He had been an itinerant photographer in California, and when he was in his sixties he began to realize that his time was running out and that he had better do something about fulfilling his life's dream, which was to sail around the world. He was quite undaunted by the fact that he knew nothing about boats or navigation, or even how to sail a boat, and also that he had very little money, certainly not enough to purchase a boat. So he simply proceeded methodically to buy a set of plans of the Seabird-type hull from the *Rudder*, to acquire building tools and materials, and to build the boat himself – to learn how to sail her, how to navigate, and finally to sail around the world, which he did not once but twice. When I got to know him in New York I was struck by his extreme modesty and self-effacement. He was no publicity hound as many adventurers are; in fact there was nothing unusual or extraordinary about what he had done, as he said to me, "I was simply enjoying myself doing what I always wanted to do." Harry's simplicity and charm endeared him to me, and we became very good friends. One day, he rather bashfully asked me if I would like to spend a weekend with him sailing his boat along the Long Island Sound. The idea did not appeal to me at all. My own boat was small but comfortable with a double stateroom, a nice galley, and full head room. Also, she was fast and handy and a pleasure to sail.

Harry's *Islander* was to me something of a tub – slow, cumbersome, poorly rigged, extremely uncomfortable down below, with little head room. However, I realized that his invitation was his idea of repaying some of the help that I had given him. So rather than hurt his feelings, I accepted and we made a rendezvous to meet in New Rochelle the following Saturday morning. Well, the day arrived and we got aboard the *Islander* at New Rochelle,

photo opposite:
Bunny at the helm

CHAPTER 10: HARRY PIDGEON

made sail, and started off. We were going to Lloyd Harbor which is only about twenty-five or thirty miles away up Long Island Sound. A nice, fresh, northwest breeze was blowing, nothing very heavy, but before we got to Larchmont, which was only about three miles away, with a crash and a bang the main gaff came running down and hit the top of the cabin. It appeared that the throat halliard had carried away. Harry, who was very unperturbed about it, said, "Oh, I'll fix that, it happens very often." So, he got a long boat hook and pulled the throat halliard block down and went below and got a piece of wire and tied it up again. We made sail and carried on. A little while later the jib sheet let go, and the jib started flogging all over the place. He said, "Oh, I will fix that," and went below, got a piece of wire and wired the jib sheet to the jib boom, and off we went again. I said to Harry, "How in heaven's name did you get around the world on this boat with all that sort of rigging?" "Oh," he said, "Before I left

California I bought a whole bale of wire, and I have used most of it already." Sure enough, everything on the boat seemed to be tied together with wire.

When we finally arrived at Lloyd Harbor we came to anchor. I said, "Harry, I think this deserves a drink. I brought a bottle of whiskey with me, so let's have a drink." "Oh," he said, "No, I don't drink. It costs money." I said, "You don't mind if I have one do you?" He said, "Oh, no, go right ahead, but I don't do anything to spend money." Of course, I knew he had no money.

After a little while I said, "Well, can I help you with the supper?" "Supper" he said, "Getting hungry?" "Well," I said, "Not very hungry, but I can eat." "Oh," he said, "I will fix that in a minute." So he went down below and in about five minutes called out, "Supper's ready." I then crawled down into this little cabin and there on the table was a loaf of bread and a dish with a lot of green things in it. I said, "What in heaven's name is that?" He said,

59

"That is bread and spinach." I said, "What are we having for supper?" He said, "That." I said, "Look Harry, I don't care much for bread and spinach and you don't care for whiskey. So why don't you eat the bread and spinach, and I will drink the whiskey." And that is how we spent the weekend at Lloyd Harbor. I had the whiskey, and he had the spinach and bread. When I asked him if that was all he ever ate, he said yes because he had the cost of living down to twenty-five cents a day. He said bread fills you up and spinach gives you strength, that's all you need. All I can say is when we got back to New Rochelle on Monday morning, I made a beeline for the nearest restaurant for a big breakfast, and then another one and still a third one. That was my weekend with Harry Pidgeon on the *Islander*.

Harry Pidgeon (August 31, 1869 - November 4, 1954)
An American sailor, a noted photographer, and was the second person to sail single-handedly around the world (1921-1925), twenty-three years after Joshua Slocum. Pidgeon was the first person to do this via the Panama Canal, and the first person to solo circumnavigate the world twice. On both trips, he sailed a thirty-four-foot yawl named the *Islander*, which Pidgeon constructed by himself. He accounts for his adventures in his book, *Around the World Single-Handed: The Cruise of the Islander* (1932).
Source: Wikipedia

In the early days of this century, before the Atomic age, before the coming of the millionaires from the north, there existed in Baltimore, Maryland, a very extraordinary club called the Free and Easy Club. It had no clubhouse and the members paid no dues, yet it was probably the most exclusive club in America. The membership was limited to twenty-five and only when a vacancy was created by a deceased member would another be elected. Even then, the qualifications for membership made it almost impossible for an outsider to get in, for a member had to be a gentleman, born and bred, and an accomplished sportsman, too. Nearly all the members were scions of old families of Maryland and Virginia whose ancestors had distinguished themselves in the various wars – the American Revolution and the Civil War, or the War between the States as they call it in Maryland. They had all been born and bred on the plantations and raised in the traditions of aristocratic country-house life.

Most of them were comparatively poor, but manners, not money, were the considered mark of a gentleman. Yet, there was nothing effeminate or soft about them. They rode hard, drank hard, and were not above a bit of whoring on the side, too. They were the sort of men who went off to war at the drop of a hat, never waiting for the rest of the nation to debate about neutrality. Many of them never came back from Flanders Fields. I thought they were the salt of the earth.

I was not a member of that Free and Easy Club, but several of its members were my close and personal friends, notably Charlie Tilghman of the Eastern Shore and Bonsal White of Green Spring Valley near Baltimore. They were all very good friends of mine and I was often invited as a guest to their parties.

The Free and Easy Club was stated to be the club formed for the perpetuation of old English sports, such as cock-fighting, bull-baiting, and rat-catching

Charles Tilghman
Descended from Dr. Richard Tilghman who, with his wife, Mary, came to America in 1660 and settled at the Hermitage in Queen Ann's County, MD. He was a highly decorated World War I captain, and a long line of Tilghmans grace the history books; Tilghman Island, MD, is their namesake.

photo opposite:
Successfully dressed Linton (right) and Bunny

CHAPTER 11: FREE AND EASY

with terriers and those sort of things. Their meetings were usually held on long weekends at the farm of one of their members out in the country.

One fine spring day when I was sitting at my desk in New York, trying to work but dreaming of my beloved Maryland, the telephone rang. It was Charlie Tilghman calling from Baltimore, urging me to come for the weekend as he said they were putting on a very good party. I arrived in Baltimore that evening and was put up at the old Baltimore Club. The next afternoon we went down to Bonny White's farm in Green Spring Valley, and I spent a few hours getting familiar with the horse I was to ride in the hunt on Saturday. That evening most of the members arrived for supper, and those suppers were really something for strong stomachs. They usually started off with Chesapeake Bay oysters – heaps of them – then soft-shelled crabs or shad roe, or something of the sort. Then usually diamondback terrapin soup well-laced with sherry, then probably pressed duck, sometimes roast beef with Yorkshire pudding, very often broiled quail or woodcock or even pheasant, and endless mint juleps. In those days nobody drank cocktails, only mint juleps and Maryland rye whiskey. After supper we retired to the stables for the ratting contest.

Now, these were something very unusual. The servants at the Baltimore Club and their friends had, for days, been catching rats in cages for the party, and there must have been four of five dozen of them brought to the farm in boxes. These were big, strong rats, not mice. Each member who owned a rat terrier brought him to the contest. For the purpose, a small circular ring with high sides had been put up, and six good rats were dropped into the ring for each contest. At the call of time an owner dropped his terrier into the ring. The terrier that killed his six rats in the shortest time was declared the winner. There was considerable betting on the bouts, and the winner collected the whole pot. It was really very good fun.

That evening we were all abed by midnight because the meet the next morning would be many miles away, and we were faced with a long early morning ride to it. The hunt on Saturday morning, as I recall it, was not very interesting. Covert after covert was drawn blank, and even the hounds were losing interest, but in the afternoon a good stout red fox was found at the very western end of the Green Spring Valley country, and away he went right off into the west to the Howard County country where hounds finally broke him up on the Doughoregan Manor Farm. It was a long point and two hours of very hard galloping, and at the end of it we were a long way from home with night coming on, and the horses were about finished. None of us felt like returning all the way to Bonny White's farm in Green Spring Valley or even to the Baltimore Club. Charlie Tilghman suggested that we all go up to Doughoregan Manor and visit Charlie Carroll who was a personal friend of his and also a member of the Free and Easy Club.

Now, the Carrolls of Carrollton had been the backbone of the Roman Catholic Church in Maryland ever since colonial days, and Doughoregan Manor was the county seat of the founders.

Doughoregan Manor was one of the most impressive country houses in that part of the world: a long, straight building with wings on both sides, a servants' quarters on one end, the family apartments in the middle, and a private chapel on the other end. Fortunately, Charlie Carroll was at home; also he was alone and happy to see us. He suggested that this was the occasion for a good party, and we agreed.

The *Ziegfeld Follies* were then playing in Baltimore and Charlie knew the manager well. He telephoned him and invited him to come out to Doughoregan Manor after the show that night and to bring some of the troupe with him. Consequently, some time after midnight a fleet of taxicabs arrived

at the manor house from Baltimore, bringing the chorus of the famous *Ziegfeld Follies*, a collection of the most beautiful young girls that you ever saw from all over America and Canada. The party was on, and what a party that was. A country band had been assembled, and there was dancing and romancing all night long. The champagne flowed freely and no one slept that night. Long before daylight, our host Charlie Carroll had passed out so we put him to bed, as I remember it, to sleep in one of his oversize bathtubs.

After breakfast the next morning, someone suggested that we ought to go fox hunting again, no doubt to show off our ability as horsemen for the benefit of the girls, several of whom claimed to be able to ride a horse. So horses were sent for as well as the hounds, which had been kept overnight in the stables. The ensuing scene on the circular grass lawn in front of the Doughoregan Manor house was one which could hardly have been duplicated except

photo opposite:
Rigg boys, Linton (center)

CHAPTER 12: FOLLIES PARTY

possibly by a Hollywood moving picture company attempting to reproduce a Roman orgy, which it must have resembled.

There were horses, hounds, grooms, servants serving drinks, handsome men – some in pink hunting clothes, others in rat catchers – beautiful disheveled girls, and much noise and laughter as they were being helped on board the horses. I must say that a pretty girl in evening dress with her skirt, pulled up some to sit on the saddle is no sight for Sunday school children.

In the middle of it all, the doors of the chapel opened and out streamed the congregation of local farmers and their families who had been attending Mass. One of our girls, a Roman Catholic, noticed that the people were carrying palm leaves and said, "Oh my God, it is Palm Sunday," and crossed herself and burst out crying. Of course, it was Palm Sunday and none of us had thought about it. The priest appeard and, of course, he was indignant. He demanded that Mr. Carroll be brought before him

and damned us all as irreligious and frivolous and guilty of indecent behavior on a sacred Sunday morning and so on. Of course, we were guilty and we tried to persuade him that it was only our fault, and that Mr. Carroll had nothing to do with it since he had gone to sleep very early. I am afraid it had little effect because we heard later that poor Charlie Carroll, on account of this party and others of a similar nature that had been held from time to time, had been excommunicated from the Church and lost his right to live in Doughoregan Manor. It was all very unfortunate.

Some ten years later I was again hunting over Doughoregan Manor lands, this time with the Howard County hounds. I was riding a horse that I had bought in Virginia for a song. I should have known there was something wrong with him, or I could never have bought him so cheaply. However, I had him vetted and he appeared to be quite sound.

On that particular day, the hounds were running fast with a breast-high scent, and it took some really bold riding to stay with them. Coming up to a very high snake fence I went at it with a considerable amount of pace. My horse, instead of rising to it, climbed right into and through it without attempting to jump at all. I was thrown into the next field and I got up with my left arm torn out of its socket and my collarbone broken. I was able to struggle back up to the manor house where Mrs. Phillip Carroll put me to bed and sent for a doctor.

Sometime later that day, after I had been strapped up and my arm pushed back into its socket, Mrs. Carroll came in to bring me a good, strong drink, which I badly needed to help stand the pain. After taking the drink and feeling a little better, I burst out laughing and she said, "What is there to laugh about? My dear man, you could have broken your neck." My reply was, "Memories." When she asked me more about them, I told her the story of the party with the *Ziegfeld Follies* girls, which had been about ten years before, and I ended up my story with, "That night, I lay in this same bed, in this same room, but not in pain, and my bedfellow was one of the most beautiful girls I have ever seen." She was very amused at all that and said, "That party became a legend around Baltimore, and I have never been able to find out who attended it and what went on. Now I know and I might as well confess it is on account of that party that my husband and I now occupy Doughoregan Manor." She was very nice to me.

Shortly after that my hunter was turned out to grass and about two or three weeks later the groom at the hunt stable, called me up and said my horse was dead. I said, "What in heaven's name happened?" He said, "He was galloping across the field and he fell into a ditch, which he didn't see and broke his neck."

It turned out that he suffered from moon blindness, which is a disease that affects some horses at certain stages of the moon and they go blind. As I look back at it, it was just pure luck he hadn't broken my neck and that was the end of my hunting in Maryland for some time.

Doughoregan Manor

The year 1928 was one of the most eventful years of my whole life and also one of the happiest. That was the year of the Transatlantic Race from New York to Spain, and it was everything a sportsman could wish for. At the beginning of the year I was looking forward to marrying a lovely girl from Virginia whom I had fallen in love with at first sight. She was a very beautiful girl of distinguished ancestry and had all the noble instincts of a lady born and bred. We were promised to each other, although our engagement had not been formally announced, but when I told her of my plan to go in the Transatlantic races, which meant being away for several months, she was beginning to have her doubts about marrying me. She had come to the conclusion that I loved boats, the sea, and adventure more than I loved her, and that she was quite convinced in her own mind that I would have never been happy living a settled sort of married life that every woman wanted. She wanted security, which I had to admit was not my line of country. I am afraid we parted tearfully. Some years later I was happy to hear that she was happily married to a good man, a steady and successful businessman in Washington, D.C., and was raising a fine brood of children.

'Isles of the Caribbees'
Carleton Mitchell, friends, and his crew, including Linton and Bunny. This picture was taken before leaving to sail the Antilles or the "Isles of the Caribbees," as Mitchell called them in his book of the same name. Mitchell took photographs and reported for National Geographic, accumulating great sailing experiences.

photo opposite:

CHAPTER 13: YEAR 1928

Well, my unhappiness did not last very long for I soon found myself entirely absorbed in the exciting preparations for the Transatlantic Race. The queen of Spain had put up a similar cup for a race for small yachts, also across the North Atlantic.

Both races were to start off at Sandy Hook in lower New York Harbor and finish in Santander, Spain, where the royal family had a summer palace. The small yachts were to start one week before the large ones. There was no difficulty in getting many entries for the large class, but the small class was quite another story. At that time it was considered quite dangerous for small yachts to race across the ocean, an idea which I think has subsequently been proven to be quite ridiculous, for a small yacht at sea is much safer than an automobile driven along the highways in modern traffic, and cruising offshore is one of the safest sports in the world. Ocean racing is only a trifle less so, the only danger is that of falling overboard or being knocked overboard at night, or a very remote chance of serious illness away from medical assistance.

The first, of course, is almost entirely eliminated nowadays by very high lifelines around the boat, which are required by the racing rules, and the crew wearing buoyant life jackets and snap-on safety belts. The latter danger, of course, can be eliminated by having the crew properly examined by a doctor before the race starts or, even better, having a doctor in the crew.

Nowadays it is not unusual for a first-class ocean racer to cost about a quarter of a million dollars or maybe even more, but in 1928 it was quite a different story. It was then considered quite fantastic to hear that Paul Hammond was spending $75,000 on building a boat especially for the race, having commissioned Starling Burgess, the famous naval architect, to design a boat to rate well under the rules, which is very necessary from the handicap point of view.

Starling Burgess …
The Burgess family and the Herreshoffs were very close and friendly. Starling, his father Edward Burgess, and Captain Nat Herreshoff (Edward's friend) designed all America's Cup winners, twelve in total, from 1885-1937.

photo opposite:
Linton racing

CHAPTER 14: OCEAN RACING

The boat Starling turned out was the *Nina*, one of the most successful ocean racers ever built with a comparatively long water line, short ends, great beam, and inside depth measurements, all factors which were favoured by the measurement rules. She got a much lower rating than most of the competitors, which were considerably smaller. Even the smaller boats had to allow her time. At that time, in the year she was built she was considered to be a rule beater. Many people called her a two-masted sloop on account of her so-called schooner rig, which gave her an additional advantage under the handicap, as she rated as a schooner although she actually had the windward going qualities of a sloop. At any rate, thirty-five years later she was still winning races, and in 1962 she cleaned up the whole modern ocean racing fleet in the race to Bermuda, which she won. She was the boat we had to try to beat, in a gaff-rigged schooner in 1928.

photo overleaf:
Carriacou sunset

photo opposite:
Linton at the helm again

My partner in business at that time was a very charming fellow, Jack Curtis, a Princeton man and fine sportsman. He was anxious to get in the race, and he suggested that he might buy a boat and go in it, but only if I would undertake and promise to fit her out for him, select a suitable crew, and to take charge of sailing her in the race. He was to be the nominal captain and I the sailing master. All that of course was right up my alley, as they say, so I readily agreed. A few days later Jack came into the office beaming and announced that he had bought the old schooner *Nicanor,* designed by John Alden, and had renamed her the *Pinta* in honour of one of Columbus' ships, as Paul Hammond had announced he was calling his new boat *Nina* also for the same reason.

I think Jack only paid about $10,000 for the *Pinta* and worst of all she was laid up in Boston, in January, frozen in ice, and the race was due to start on July 4th. I had a sinking feeling that we were jinxed from the start for there is a very strong superstition among seamen that it is very bad luck to change the name of a boat. In the case of the *Pinta* I was certain it was proved because we lost the Transatlantic Race. Subsequently, when she was being loaded on board a freighter in France to be shipped back to America, she was dropped by the crane and badly damaged. When she arrived in Boston and was unloaded, she was moored between two ships, one of which broke loose and poor old *Pinta* was crushed between them, damaged again. Somewhat later in her career, after having been repaired and put into commission again, she started off on a cruise to the West Indies, and on that cruise she was run aground on the beach off Cape Hatteras and had to be pulled off by the Coast Guard and towed into Norfolk, Virginia. Later, on another cruise, she caught fire and was very badly damaged. Eventually, she was abandoned in Hamilton Harbour, Bermuda, and was taken out to sea and

John Gale Alden (1884 – 1962) …
Founder of Alden Designs, a prominent yacht design company. His designs were inspired by docked Grand Banks fishing schooners that he saw in 1900.. Alden worked under yacht designer Edward Burgess and later for his son, Starling Burgess, both of whom designed America's Cup yachts. At one point, Starling shared an office with Linton in New York City.
Source: Wikipedia

photo opposite:
Racing team Linton 3nd from right, Bunny on his right

CHAPTER 15: PINTA

sunk by the Harbour authorities.

But to get back to the races: First of all we had to get the *Pinta* down from Boston where she was frozen up and bring her to New York where we could work on her. As every ocean racing man knows, six months is hardly time enough to convert an old cruising boat into a seagoing ocean racer. First of all, of course the hull, deck, houses and spars all had to be gone over with a fine-toothed comb and searched for weaknesses and made like new. Then the endless problems of sails and rigging, spare parts for everything, etc., etc., item for item, also the provisioning of the vessel, were serious things. You have to carry enough food, water and all the other necessary supplies for a large ocean racing crew over a couple of months. That alone is a job that required much thought and very careful planning.

I do remember that on July 4th when we were finally towed out to the starting line off Sandy Hook we were still working on her. It seems that no ship is ever a hundred percent ready to go to sea. What you have to do is to set a date and a time and then go, ready or not. Just before casting off to go to the starting line Lank Ford's mother came alongside in a boat, which she had chartered to bring some final instructions and supplies, among which was a roll of oil cloth that she gave him with instructions to be sure to put it over his bed to keep it dry because, as she said, "Now son, you must always remember that you catch a cold when you sleep in a wet bed." Well, we found that very amusing, but that particular piece of cloth proved to be the most useful thing we had on board. I doubt if any of us slept in a dry bunk all the way across, for old *Pinta* whenever she rolled, and she rolled plenty, slapped all the bilge water into the bunks, and she leaked continually. Some three weeks later, when we were struggling through a gale in the Bay of Biscay, a very heavy sea broke on board and shifted the whole cabin house about an inch from its original position. After that, every sea that came on board poured water into the cabin below. Ever-resourceful Lank Ford unrolled his oil cloth and rigged up an ingenous set of gutters leading to buckets that relieved us of much of the back-breaking pumping. Any boat is unsinkable as long as you keep the water out of it.

Shamrock III rounding lightboat

The race across was great fun, and after the first day we saw no other boat for three weeks, and in order to keep the crew really sharp we raced watch against watch. We drove them pretty hard night and day, always having the *Nina* in mind. One of the other boats in the race, the *Rover*, was dismasted. A steamer picked her up and attempted to give her a tow but she sank while she was being towed. That was really the only casualty of the race, and no man was lost at any time. We had wonderful weather – strong southwest winds – and one day we logged 256 nautical miles from noon to noon, which I think is pretty much of a record for a forty-two-foot water line boat. We must have had some current with us to enable us to do that, as we still pretty much on the edges of the Gulf Stream which, as we all know, runs all the way to the coast of Europe. Then, when we made our land fall at Cape Ortegal on the coast of Spain, a sail could be sighted on the horizon behind us, which was very cheerful, and a cheer went up from the crew as she was identified through the glasses as the *Nina*. In other words, we had outsailed *Nina* across the ocean, and we were feeling pretty cocky about that, but not for long. The wind was dying out and hauling ahead, and soon we were hard on wind – very light air – and under those conditions the best that *Pinta* could make good was six points off the wind. With the finish only a few miles away, the *Nina* sailed by us holding about two points higher and moving so fast that we looked foolish. Of course, those were the very conditions for which she had been designed, so she won easily.

Shamrock V
The first British yacht to be built to the new J-Class rule. She was commissioned by Sir Thomas Lipton for his fifth (and ultimately last) America's Cup challenge. Although restored many times she is the only J not to have ever fallen into dereliction.
Source: Wikipedia

photo opposite:

CHAPTER 16: THE RACE

In Spain we had a ball, in fact, I might say we had several balls. King Alfonso, a yachtsman himself, proved to be a perfect host. He visited all the yachts, one after the other, talking to us in a democratic way. He seemed quite envious of our democratic ways and freedom of the stiffness, which affected most of the people in his presence. I remember the amusing remark he made that he would rather be president of General Motors Corporation in America than king of Spain.

On the second day after our arrival we were all invited to a dance at the palace that night. There were hundreds of people at the dance, and the ballroom was crowded. In the interval between dances, I found myself standing near the king. I walked over to him and told him that I had a personal letter to him from Freddy Prince introducing me and that I had hoped to deliver it the next day. To this he said, "Well, that shall not be necessary. If you are a friend of Freddy Prince, you are a personal friend of mine, so now we must have a drink together." Whereupon, he took me by the arm and we walked to the dining room. Of course, as soon as the king moved the music stopped, the couples parted, and as we walked through the crowd, I felt very conspicuous and wished that I could drop through the floor. However, it was so natural that I was soon relaxed, and we proceeded to tell each other stories about yachting and fox hunting, which he loved. He had often gone to Pau in the south of France and stayed with Freddy Prince who kept a pack of hounds there; also, he played polo with Freddy. I remember one amusing story that he told me about a visit he made to England incognito.

He was out one night, night clubbing with the prince of Wales, both on the hunt for a little feminine companionship. After picking up a pair of likely-looking girls they set off in two cabs, one by the prince being urged to drive fast, and the one with the king and his girl trying to keep up with the prince. In

Freddy Prince (1859-1953)
As member of the New York Yacht Club he owned the *Weetamoe*, a J class yacht, competing for a berth in the Americas Cup, losing in the 1934 trials to the ultimate Cup winner Harold Sterling Vanderbilt and his yacht, *Rainbow*. He made a fortune through his investments in a number of business ventures, owned Armor and Company, railroads, and was a friend of Joseph Kennedy all the while aiding President Franklin Roosevelt's efforts to pull America out of the Great Depression.
Source: Wikipedia

photo opposite:
Linton down the hatch

CHAPTER 17: SPAIN

84

doing so, the driver of the king's cab hit the curb at Hyde Park corner; the cab turned over and spilled the king and the girl onto the pavement. No one was hurt, fortunately, but up came the inevitable London bobby with his notebook, "Sorry about all this, sir. I am glad no one is hurt, but I am afraid I must take your name and the lady's too." "Oh very well officer," said the king, "I am the king of Spain." With a sort of annoyed look the bobby then said, "Now look here my man, none of that nonsense, what is your real name?", to which the king replied "Alfonso, King of Spain." The bobby then showed irritation which is unusual for a London bobby and said "Look here, I have had enough of these games. Ever since the king of Spain arrived here last week, every tipsy fool says I am the king of Spain. Now my man, what is your real name? I ask you for the last time." The king replied, "Alfonso, King of Spain." "Well, come and tell that to the Sergeant that you are the king of Spain and see what he has to say." At the stationhouse the sergeant took one look and said, "For God's sake let him go before we get into trouble. He is the king of Spain."

There were other amusing incidents. In honour of the occasion of our arrival there was quite a collection of warships in the harbour, both Spanish and American. One night there was a big dance on one of the battleships, and I danced quite a lot with Princess Maria Cristina. She was a very charming girl.

In the middle of one of the dances she said to me, "Please, Mr. Rigg, take me outside quickly." Of course, I thought she had probably dropped her pants or something, so I quickly maneuvered her out into a quiet spot away from the dance. When we got there, she laughingly explained that when we were dancing she had pinched a Naval officer on his bottom as we were dancing past him. Then she looked up to see that he was one of the American officers, not a Spanish one, much to her embarrassment. After a while, the queen sent one of her ladies-in-waiting to find us and asked me please not to monopolize the princess so much and to bring her back into the ballroom, which I had to do.

photo overleaf:
Carriacou pelican

photo opposite:
Linton staying cool

A few mornings later, Lank Ford and I were having breakfast at the Royal Yacht Club when we noticed that all the people in the dining room were suddenly standing up. Looking around for the reason, we saw that the king was entering the room and he made his way directly to our table. Then we realized that he had come to see us.

Now on that morning on the way to breakfast, walking through the town, Lank Ford had spotted about a dozen fresh eggs, which he was now carrying in a paper bag. As the king came towards us and stopped at our table, we stood up and Lank automatically rose, holding the paper bag in his hands. Of course, the eggs must have been kept cool in water or something, for the bottom of the bag dropped out and a dozen eggs burst right at the feet of the king.

When that little inconvenience had been cleared up, the king said, "Mr. Rigg, I have come to ask you to play polo with me this afternoon." After a moment's thought, I said, "I am very sorry, your majesty, but I am afraid I can't possibly do it today, maybe at another time." "Ay," he said, "May I ask why?" I said, "Yes sir, I am very sorry but I have made another appointment." "Well," said the king, "You must cancel it." I said, "I am very sorry sir, but it would be impossible." The king's eyebrows went up and he said, "Why not, send a message and say that you are playing polo with the king this afternoon." I had a very embarrassing job to explain to the king that my engagement was with a lady whom I had met at the palace and that we had arranged to meet at the country club that afternoon, which is a long way out in the country. She was to get horses, and we were to go for a long ride. "Then send her a message," he said. "She will understand that you must play polo with the king." I had further embarrassment to explain that I could not possibly send her a message because I didn't know her name. Then he said, "You don't know her name at all?" I

photo opposite:
Necessary provisions

CHAPTER 18: THE KING

said, "I only know her Christian name; I don't know her last name." That seemed to annoy him because in a rather sarcastic tone he said, "Ah, so you prefer to go riding with a lady who has no name. Very well, Mr. Rigg," and he turned away.

The duke of Alba who was with him, came up to me and said, " I am sorry, Mr. Rigg, but if the king asks you to play polo with him you have to play polo with him – you cannot refuse. It is not done." To which I replied, "I am very sorry, sir, but I cannot do so. I have already told the king why and I think he understands." To which the duke of Alba said, "But you cannot do that." I said, "My dear sir, I have already done it, and that is the end of it as far as I am concerned." He turned away saying rather scornfully, "I cannot understand you Americans."

Well, I thought I was very much finished as far as hospitality at the palace was concerned, but the next night was a formal dinner, given at the palace in our honour. I had to attend and after dinner the king walked up to me and said, "Well, Mr. Rigg, how did you enjoy your ride with the lady who has no name?" I said, "Very much, sir. It was a very welcome change from the sea, and I found the lady quite pleasant indeed, quite pleasant." He looked at me with a smile and said, "Yes, I know all about that; you have good taste in women it would seem." So, I was apparently forgiven. I found out later that she, the woman, a lovely girl too, was one of his favorite illegitimate children.

Later that same night we were to see the other side of the coin, and it was not very pretty. A Spanish yachtsman offered to take us on a tour of the red light district, and Dudley Wolfe and I went with him. Now in my opinion, the red light district is a very essential part of the large shipping ports of the world. Traveling men, especially men of the sea, who are often away from normal contacts with women for months at a time, are essentially very lonely men, especially in foreign ports where they know no one and often cannot even speak the language. Also, in a red light district, and only in a red light district, do they find feminine companionship immediately and without delay and without formality of introduction. Also, the women of the red light district are trained in all arts on pleasing men and satisfying their natural appetites. I think it might well be said that although they are not the most desirable women, they are at least much better than no women at all. Most of the women who enter that sort of life do so because they enjoy the excitement and find it the easiest way to make money. The only really sad part of it, I think, is the occasional young girls who are forced into it, and I think that is pretty awful. That night, we saw little girls being kept locked up in a bedroom with all their clothes taken away from them so they could not escape. Little girls, some of them only children twelve to fifteen years old, awaiting shipment to the brothels of South America.

One particularly beautiful girl, whom we were told was brought from Poland, lay in bed quite naked, being kept under lock and key all the time, awaiting shipment to South America. Although she could not speak English, her sad eyes gestured, indicating that she was pleading with us to rescue her. Dudley Wolfe, who was quite wealthy, suggested that he would buy her and then release her, but the woman in charge said that was impossible. She had already been sold for $1,000 to a brothel keeper in Buenos Aires. The thought of what that child would have to endure at the hands of forty or fifty uncouth men every night, possibly for the rest of her life, just made us sick at heart. As Dudley and I walked back to the yacht club that night, we turned to each other and said, "Well, that just about finishes Spain for me. I am disgusted with it. This inhumanity is really more than I could bear." We made our farewells to the palace and we sailed in Dudley's schooner *Mohawk*, for the clean, cool air of England.

Dudley Wolfe
In her book, *Last Man on the Mountain: The Death of an American Adventurer on K2*, Jennifer Jordan, an award-winning author, filmmaker and screenwriter, writes that Wolfe was a rich American in 1939. He was very unassuming, very quiet, a very gentle adventurous soul. He was always an athlete, from his early prep school days right straight through to his death. And he was a man who looked at life to be explored and to really get out there and see things that no one else had seen. As a yacht racer he joined the Queen's Cup race from New York to Spain. On *Mohawk*, his sixty-foot schooner, he also crossed the Atlantic in the mid '20s.

This is a story of the America's Cup and how it was almost lost. It was July 1962, the year that the Australians had challenged for the cup and come up from Down Under with the *Gretel*, a very fast boat, with the idea of trying to win the America's Cup. I was, at that time, staying in the New York Yacht Club. The publishers of my book, *The Alluring Antilles*, had urged me to come up from the West Indies, as they wanted me to go over the manuscript very carefully with them. I am not a member of the New York Yacht Club, but Mr. Eugene Connett, the editor of the Van Nostrand Company, is a member. He suggested that I should stay at the club for many reasons, one being the fact that it was not very far away from his office in New York City; the other one was that if I needed any research in connection with my book, the New York Yacht Club had a very excellent library, and since he was a member, he arranged to put me up. I had a very nice room up on the third floor, a room which had been occupied for

many years by my old friend, Sherman Hoyt.

It was a very comfortable little room at the back of the club – very quiet and a good place to work. There were very few people staying at the club at the time because most of the yachtsmen had already left for Newport and the others were off cruising. The Australians were in and out of town all the time. They had the *Gretel* up at Newport but they were down in New York frequently, getting equipment and copying everything they could see on the American boat. In honour of their visit, the America's Cup had been brought from Tiffany's vault and was on display in the model room of the yacht club.

I spent about a week or ten days going over the manuscript for my book, trying to add a few little personal touches, very much against my desire, but the publishers insisted that I put in a few of my personal experiences to make the book more readable, which I proceeded to do.

Shortly before my intended departure, the

Eugene Connett
During the 1920s Eugene Connett lived in Long Island and was a member of the Piping Rock Club and the Bellport Yacht Club. He was a member of Princeton's Class of 1912. Prior to founding his own imprint, The Derrydale Press, Connett did commission design and book production for well-heeled Eastern bibliophiles like himself, including the likes of Mark Twain's works; many of his editions now fetch fortunes on the rare book markets.

photo opposite:
Linton's photo of a 'grey beard', a wave at sea

CHAPTER 19: NEW YORK YACHT CLUB

librarian of the club came to me one day and said he heard that I was writing a book about the Caribbean, possibly for yachtsmen. He wanted to know if he could help me in any way and if he had any information that would be of value to me. I said I thought that I had collected everything that I knew because I had spent three years cruising all around the West Indies, some of them several times, but there was one historical matter that I had never been able to get to the bottom of.

The Battle of the Saints was, in my opinion, one of the most wonderful sea battles ever fought, and I think that in some ways it is equally as important as the Battle of Trafalgar. I had never been able to read in any of the current books a seaman-like account of that battle; the sort of things in which a seaman is naturally interested: the weather conditions, the winds, the sea, the deployment of the fleets, the tactics, and also the conclusion formed after the engagement. All these were things of great interest to me because I had cruised in those waters several times and had tried to imagine the conditions that had existed during the battle. Much to my surprise, about two days later he sent up to my room nine or ten books, all about the Battle of the Saints. Well, to me it was a gold mine of information because there were three or four of them that I think were the official Admiralty accounts of the battle.

Two of them were books written by Lord Rodney. One of them, as I recall it, was a book written by Hood, and the others were all books written at a contemporary date about the battle and its results and the political aftermath of the battle. I was so fascinated with these books that I prolonged my stay at the yacht club for another week. I read day and night until I was through the whole lot of them. As a result, I was able to write most of the things, the important things that interested me personally, and boil them down into one or two pages in my book.

Now the Battle of the Saints had tremendous

historical effect on the whole western world, and the events that lead up to it are not often spoken of or are certainly not told in American schools. I have been able to put together a couple of things as a result of my reading those books. One of them was the fact that the American colony actually won their independence through the help of the French, much more so than the school histories have taught in the United States, to give you an idea. Of course, every nation at war with another nation naturally endeavors to seize an opportunity to stab another one in the back if possible. The British at that time were actually at war with the French, the Spanish, and the Dutch. The French were the principal opponents. Now, the French were quite unable to handle the British fleet in European waters so they naturally seized the opportunity, when the American colonies revolted, to literally stab the British in the back by joining the Americans in the colonies. To do that, they outfitted a tremendous fleet under Admiral de Grasse and sent it to the American coast to blockade Chesapeake Bay, where Cornwallis was being besieged by the American forces under George Washington.

I think it was unquestionably a fact that it was the blockading by de Grasse of the British Army and Yorktown that necessitated the surrender of Cornwallis. He couldn't be supplied, he couldn't be relieved, and he couldn't be helped in any way because the French fleet had blockaded Chesapeake Bay; the British naval forces in America at that time were quite inferior to the French fleet and couldn't break the blockade.

Not long ago I was reading a book published quite recently about the actual figures of the two armies. It turned out that at the time of Cornwallis' surrender at Yorktown, George Washington's army only comprised thirty-five hundred regular soldiers and two thousand militia, a total army of five thousand five hundred men. At the same time the

---

Battle of the Saints
The battle is famous for the innovative tactic of "breaking the line," in which the British ships passed though a gap in the French line, engaging the enemy from leeward and throwing them into disorder. As the French line passed down the British line, a sudden shift of wind let Rodney's flagship *Formidable* break through the French line, raking the ships as they did so. The result: confusion in the French line and severe damage to several of the French ships including de Grasse's flagship. But there is considerable controversy about whether the tactic was intentional, and, if so, who was responsible for the idea; all was just the type of maritime history that floated Linton's boat.
Source: Wikipedia

French had over nine thousand troops on the land fighting and something like twenty-two thousand men on the ships of the fleet, a total number of over thirty-one thousand men altogether, compared to Washington's less than six thousand. I think the American people never really realized how much they owe to the French nation for their delivery from British rule. Well, of course, the French having accomplished the defeat of the British on American soil quite naturally felt that they had the British on the run and all they thought it was necessary to do. The complete determination of British Colonial rule in the Western Hemisphere was to go down and capture the West Indies, particularly Jamaica, which at that time was the richest colony in the British Empire. Therefore, de Grasse was ordered back to France and was ordered to assemble a very large fleet and an army of something like fifteen thousand men on transports with mobile artillery landing forces and troops to be landed in Jamaica. Then he sailed for the conquest of the West Indies, or so he thought.

Admiral Rodney set out from England to try and stop that, and he collected a British fleet in St. Lucia. The rest of the story, of course, is history. De Grasse and his fleet were trying to mix in with the Spanish fleet in Cuba, and Rodney's job was to try to stop them from doing that. When de Grasse finally sailed from Martinique headed for Cuba, Rodney pursued him. It is a long story of all the things that led up to the battle. Finally their forces met at the little group of islands just south of Guadeloupe and there the Battle of the Saints was fought. To read all the official Admiralty reports on the battle and all the other things that were written at the time was a fascinating job for me. I just couldn't put them down, but finally after about a week or ten days, I finished and I prepared to leave.

photo opposite:
Sailors' celebration

On the morning of my departure I was up very early and spent about an hour reading over, for the final time, the manuscript of the book on which I had been working for three years. That was a very important piece of paper for me, and I was determined that there would not be one tiny mistake in it anywhere. Having satisfied myself on that point, I walked down to the office of the publisher which was on West Fortieth Street just five blocks away from the yacht club. I arrived there at eight o'clock intending to give the manuscript to the secretary of the editor, and much to my dismay I found that the office was locked. I had already arranged to take a train from Grand Central Station at, I think it was about 9:30. I knew that I wouldn't have time to wait and deliver the manuscript and get back to the yacht club and have breakfast and catch the train. In desperation, I left my precious manuscript with a strange elevator man I had never seen in my life, and I gave him a few dollars and trusted that he would deliver the papers to the office when it opened, and I went off.

I then walked back leisurely to the yacht club and had breakfast, and I must say that the breakfast at the New York Yacht Club was without parallel anywhere in New York City. The service was wonderful and the food excellent. After breakfast, I took the elevator up to my room on the third floor. I put the key in the door and as I opened the door, a tremendous cloud of smoke rushed out at me and flames, it would seem, were stretching right up to the ceiling of my room.

I was never so frightened in my life. It took me only a few seconds to realize that the whole New York Yacht Club would be in flames within the next few minutes unless something was done about it. Having opened the door and created a draught which fanned the flames even more, my first thought was to rush to the window and open it. I realized that would be fatal, for that would create a further draught. Then I desperately tried to think what to

photo opposite:
New York Yacht Club © CarolRossPhotography.com

CHAPTER 20: FIRE

do. I should call for help, but I realized that before help could come the whole place would be on fire, and I couldn't wait for a fire engine or any other help from the outside. I had to put that fire out myself, which I proceeded to do. It took me about half an hour; I was blinded by smoke, I could hardly breathe and the flames were licking at my face all the time. My eyebrows were singed off and my skin was scorched, but I eventually put the fire out. I smothered it with my jacket, I beat it with my hands, and finally I had it out sufficiently so that I could stagger over to the wash basin, fill a jug with water, and pour it on the remains and make sure that it was permanently out. There was a great hole in the floor; the desk was consumed, as were the curtains and everything else in the room. It was in a horrible mess and when I looked at my watch I saw that I only had about fifteen minutes to catch my train at Grand Central Station.

I went out and I must have looked like a tramp staggering out of the chimney or something, grabbed my bags and not waiting for the elevator, ran down the steps, left word at the door with the doorman about what happened, and ran over to Grand Central Station. I found that it was only about two or three minutes away from the time for my train to leave, so I ran to the ticket window and found that a long line of people had queued up for tickets. It was hopeless to try to get a ticket so I turned around and ran back to the gate where the guard tried to stop me. I had to push him aside and run for the train. I got on board just as the doors were closing. As I sank down in my seat, I realized that I had come within just a few minutes of probably being the most hated man in the yachting world or even in yachting history, probably as much despised as the man who shot Abraham Lincoln. For, undoubtedly, through some carelessness of mine, probably a cigarette butt or an unextinguished match thrown into the waste paper basket, I had almost demolished the New York Yacht

Club with the finest collection of yacht models in the world, one of the finest yachting libraries in the world, and the America's Cup. When I got to Newport, I wrote a complete account of the whole affair and sent it with a letter reporting the matter, and with an accompanying letter sent it to the New York Yacht Club expressing my regret and apology and offering to pay for the repairs to the damage to the yacht club.

I received a very nice letter in reply from Mr. Whiting, chairman of the House Committee, in which he said that the danger of fire to the New York Yacht Club had been of his chief worries every since he took over the job as chairman of the House Committee. He thanked me profusely for having put out the fire and said nothing of my culpability and ended up with very good news that the cost of repairing the damage was completely covered by fire insurance that was carried by the yacht club. So ended that most frightening affair.

Sailing under History, The Brooklyn Bridge, NYC
© CarolRossPhotography.com

The match races for the cup, which was sailed in September of that year, were more than ordinarily interesting, I think, because the two boats and also their crews were so very evenly matched. The production of a winning boat in a class as closely restricted as the twelve metres is largely a matter of evolution I think. The successful designer is usually the one with an exhaustive collection of data based on the performance of a progressive series of boats, each one a little better than the other, improving the design as he goes along. The Australians had gotten around that handicap by chartering the *Vim* which was one of Olin Stephens' most successful twelve metre designs. They took her to Australia, took her lines off and thus captured much of the data compiled by Olin Stephens over a period of years. With that in hand, it was not too difficult to plan a few advances in design, which I think had already become obvious to students in naval architecture. In addition, in that year, through the courtesy of the New York Yacht Club Committee, the Australians were allowed the privilege of copying many of the improvements that they saw on the American boats.

J. Linton Rigg

photo overleaf:
2004 Carriacou Regatta race start, author aboard race winner *Yellowbird*

photo opposite:
Under sail, local built work boat, Carriacou

CHAPTER 21: AMERICA'S CUP

Tropic of Cancer

North Atlantic
Ocean

Turks &
Caicos

Dominican
Republic

US/British
Virgin Islands

Saint Martin

Barbuda

Antigua

Puerto Rico

Montserrat

Guadeloupe

Dominica

Sea

Martinique

St. Lucia

Barbados

St. Vincent

Aruba

Curacao

The Grenadines

Carriacou

Grenada

Bonaire

Tobago

mbia

Venezuela

The Bermuda Race

It's easy to see how Linton came up with his ideas about starting regattas. From the sweet cup of sailing his family had nurtured him to drink, and he would never be free of its taste.

Any story of a man, a sailor like Linton, would be incomplete without some explanation regarding racing. Simply stated, anytime two boats are within sight of one another the first thing a yachtsman considers is "can we beat that boat." Not that this was restricted to then only because it's much the same now as well. As a result, the defining character of a man was that he raced. When Linton was a young man, his memoirs point that out clearly. As he got older, he got better, becoming one of the very best.

When he was only a child fishing in Wilmington, Delaware, the Bermuda Race was started by Linton's friend, Thomas Fleming Day, in 1906. Day thought that sailors wanted to forget the times when they smelled the earth and wanted only the smell of the seas. As a skipper, Fleming won the first Bermuda Race – started from New York (Brooklyn) – aboard the *Tamerlane*, a thirty-eight-foot yawl. Later the race sailed every other year over a 635-mile course from Newport, Rhode Island, to St. David's Head, Bermuda, now one of the largest ocean races with fleets larger than 170 boats. It's affectionately called the "Thrash to the Onion Patch" because it usually includes sailing in rough water, crossing the Gulf Stream and hundreds of miles of open Atlantic Ocean, finishing at a small island that was long an agricultural center, Bermuda.

In 1923 *Yachting* magazine rejuvenated the race with the purpose of encouraging the designing, building, and sailing of small seaworthy yachts. It was to make popular cruising upon deep water and to develop in the amateur sailor a love of true seamanship – to give an opportunity to become proficient in the art of navigation. Since 1926 the Bermuda Race has been co-organized by the Cruising Club of America (founded 1922) and the Royal Bermuda Yacht Club (founded 1845).

Linton's old friend Carleton Mitchell was an avid racer. When he died at the seasoned age of 96 in 2007, it was said of him by his friend, that Mitchell was really a three-sport star – a sailor, a photographer and a writer, one of the best of all time. He had competed in many races and won the Bermuda Race three times consecutively in *Finisterre*, a feat never accomplished by anyone else.

photo opposite:
Building a boat the old way in Windward, Carriacou 2004

THE BAHAMA ISLANDS

Scale: Nautical Miles

Note: Map not to be used for navigation

N / W / E / S

Walker Cay
West End
Grand Bahama
Great Isaac
Green Turtle Cay
Man-O-War Cay
Hopetown
ABACO

Bimini
Gun Cay
Cat Cay
N.W. CHANNEL LT.
The Berry Is.
Harbour Is.
NASSAU
ELEUTHERA

Great Bahama Bank
ANDROS
The Exuma Cays
EXUMA SOUND
CAT IS.
Conception Is.
WATLINGS or SAN SALVADOR
Rum Cay
TROPIC OF CANCER
GREAT EXUMA IS.
Long Is.
Crooked Is. Passage
Atwood Cay
CROOKED IS.
The Jumentos Cays
MAYAGUANA IS.
ACKLINS IS.
Cay Lobos
Ragged Is.
Castle Is.
Hogsty Reef
Little Inagua
THE CAICOS IS.

CUBA
Santiago
GREAT INAGUA
TORTUGA
Cap Haitien
The Windward Passage
HAITI
DOMI

The Out Island Race

Linton and Bunny were expert helmsmen. And being terrific seamen they shared more similarities than differences with the people of the Bahamas. Howland Bottomley, commodore emeritus, described the working sail as fast disappearing from their part of the world in the 1950s, commenting, "The Grand Banks fishing schooner was all but gone, the Chesapeake Oystermen were no longer being replaced as they were laid up, and the many vessels still working under canvas in the Bahamas had an uncertain future." In 1954 Linton and a group of Bahamian yachtsmen conceived the idea of holding a regatta for the Bahamian working sailing craft.

Bottomley noted, "The overall condition of the working fleet was not good, and it was felt that the material condition of the boats would be improved by the preparations necessary to ready the vessels for racing competition. A regatta would also offer a fine opportunity for Bahamian sailors to all gather in one place, have some sport, and a chance for cruising yachtsmen to witness one of the last working sailing fleets in action. At the same time introduce them all to the magnificent cruising grounds here in The Bahamas." At this point, Linton's vision was in its early stages.

So in the year 1954, Great Exuma welcomed its very first regatta, now called the National Family Island Regatta. Linton conceived of the race and was chairman of the race committee. At the first race he made the late announcement that the starting time had been extended an hour, and the first race would be started at two o'clock. Despite this, some ships did not arrive in time to participate in the race. A short time later, the committee changed the race course and the run was held inside the harbor instead of around Stocking Island as originally planned. This kept the smaller craft out of the rough waters of the open ocean. The first race, over a four-mile triangular course, combined large and intermediate-class work boats. The latter course was a three-mile run inside the harbor. Saturday, the same courses were run twice again. First prize in each class was one hundred pounds with fifty pounds for second, twenty-five pounds for third and ten pounds for fourth. In addition, special prizes were awarded in a variety of dinghy races.

While the bigger craft, divided into two classes, lumbered off into Exuma harbor, thirty smaller and speedier dinghies formed a breathtaking sight as they started their three-mile jaunt. The shores and the Government Dock were lined with crowds of enthusiastic spectators. Out in the harbor, either following the fleet or anchored in full view of the races, were close to forty visiting yachts. Today the event is the year's largest tourist draw and has hundreds of yachting participants. The Bahamian wooden sailing vessel has served the Bahamas for many years gone by, and will continue to do so

thanks in part to Linton's great idea back in 1954. Now the boat-building skills that helped sustain this nation in the past are alive and well to serve it in the future.

There is a later story of Linton from about the time he "went island" as it was whispered about, as told by a number of those who knew him well. After his marriage to a rich debutante socialite who hailed from Charleston, South Carolina, whom it was believed he'd met in Annapolis, there were suspicions that the reason he left New York and abandoned his yacht sales career was because his family life was falling apart. At that time he was a rich and successful yacht broker. It is said that he went to Windsor Castle and played polo there on the grounds, and that later due to his association with Prince Philip, he was able to convince Philip to come and attend one of the early Out Islands Regattas. In any case, his marriage produced a child and at a time when his daughter was four or five, his wife implored him to allow her to go home to Charleston in order to visit her mother. Linton made all the arrangements. His wife and daughter boarded a train at Penn Station in New York City and he never saw them again! Pinkerton detectives later determined that the two got off the train in Jersey City and met an unidentifiable man, got on a ship, and sailed to Paris. Linton tried in particular to get in contact with his daughter, but accounts indicate he never saw her again. Some were to say he was a horrible husband, overbearing, sexist, and a misogynist. He seems to have considered females as a lesser species. He never referred to this loss in his writings.

Linton and Bunny spent some time in Nassau after ocean races, and there got to see the fleet of native craft. Later Linton cruised the Bahamas on several occasions in *Chinquapin*, his motorsailor and wrote up the first cruising guide of the Bahamas. During that time he did talk with native men about sailboat racing, and was known to have recommended that they have some racing fun. But it would have come to nothing were it not for Ward Wheelock. Ward Wheelock was a successful advertising executive who lived in a mansion on the Mainline, near Philadelphia. He had the national Campbell Soup account and the Hershey Company account. After World War II he got involved with charitable causes, including the Eisenhower Educational fellowships. He was appalled at the use of the atomic bomb and dedicated his life to work for world peace and racial harmony. Wheelock was very well connected; he knew everyone of importance in America. He founded something he called "Help, Inc." which funded charitable works.

He is best known for coming up with the incredibly popular radio program and later the book, *This I Believe*. These were five-minute interview pieces with famous people narrated by Edward R. Murrow; *This I Believe* would become Murrow's

'Mermaid of Carriacou' launch day

signature work. Eventually as the program got to be enormously popular and ran on a daily schedule, Murrow broadened his approach to interesting common men. One of these men was Linton Rigg.

Wheelock sailed on a cruise to George Town, Exuma, to meet with Linton and record a five-minute segment for *This I Believe*. The transcript of Linton's segment makes him out to be a very pious and ethical man. His segment was about why a man would abandon fame and success to leave New York and go live at the ends of the earth, in a place with only a few white people and fewer still, people of his own level of education. He made a very eloquent case for doing this, but at no point does he own up to the problems with his family and what part that may have played in his decision to stay in the islands.

It was Ward Wheelock who really made the idea of a regatta work. While on that visit he told Linton that if he would do the local work, he (Wheelock) would find a way to come up with the money. Wheelock didn't attend the first Out Island Regatta in 1954, being too busy with his advertising business and an ailing wife. His wife died soon thereafter and he again married a sailor, and together they were determined to see the second regatta. They flew to Bermuda with a son and some friends, bound eventually for George Town and the regatta. They left Bermuda on the Wheelock family schooner, *HSH,* and all were lost at sea. A huge search was undertaken but only a life vest was eventually found. In the end of his time in the Bahamas Linton had owned some of the finest real estate in the Exumas, no doubt providing him with the seed money to head down island.

Island Belle drying sails taken from Linton's book 'Alluring Antilles" (1963)

photo opposite:
Bones of island boat building

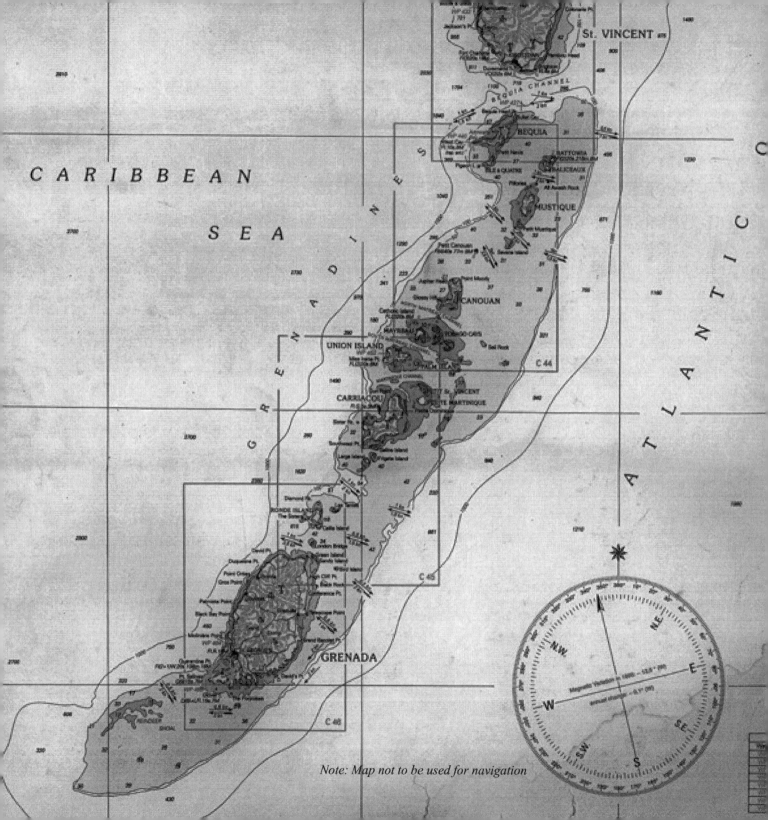

Note: Map not to be used for navigation

The Carriacou Regatta

From the mariner's prospective J. Linton Rigg died a noble death, having left them a legacy – a boost to their boat-building industry and all recreational sailing to come. His contribution was the iconic idea of regattas, which has grown and blossomed, and advanced to different stages of maturity through many years. As successive regattas are celebrated, Linton's memory remains very much in the spotlight. He was almost a seventy-year-old man when he came to this small thirteen-square-mile island. He had been in many Bermuda races and on Transatlantic races, and he held many prominent positions: He was a yacht broker, he owned his own businesses and he commissioned from the best in the States, from Alden to Hinckley. He was chairman of the Board of Small Vessels for the United States during World War II, stationed in Washington, D.C., while Bunny was a heroic USCG skipper in the war effort. He was a very senior member of the Royal Ocean Racing Club of London, England, and the Royal Nassau Sailing Club of Nassau Bahamas. At age sixty-five he left the Bahamas to cruise the entire Caribbean on his boat *The Island Belle*, writing his next cruising guide.

After the depth of his exploration, he chose as his paradise, Carriacou, in the Grenadine Islands – a haven of peace. He established the Mermaid Tavern and became a hotelier.

It was not long and no real surprise after his arrival in 1960 that he had the great idea of organizing a Carriacou Regatta, and in 1965 he laid down plans for his first event. He wrote letters, broadcasting publicity by press and radio. He gathered support in the form of naval vessels from local governments and money from merchant associates as well as anyone else within his voice or pen. Promoting the proposed regatta, he traveled to Bequia in the north and Grenada in the south, along the way meeting many of those sailors who later participated in the races; many still remember him as the leader that he was.

He had his frustrating moments when plans on the island seemed not to be taking the right course,

chart opposite:
Grenadine Islands

THE RACES: THE CARRIACOU REGATTA

but with the able assistance of the local authorities he eventually found himself on Saturday, August 1, 1965, starting off the first race from Grenada's southern end. The first yacht *Flica* entered the Hillsborough harbour in Carriacou and in its wake carrying the challenge posed to yachts over the years to come. The outcome of the first Carriacou Regatta was indeed a success, which paved the way for the institution it has become.

He wanted to put Carriacou on the map by encouraging the boat building of more and faster working sailboats, and to give the sailors and yachtsmen a chance to mix. At the same time, he would promote his tavern business. By 1968 he had a great regatta going on. Competition was fierce; the most successful boat builder, Zepherine McLaren, and he built jointly the sloop *Mermaid or Carriacou*. With the regatta well on the way, the government took over and Linton grudgingly passed on the responsibility, though he did go on to race and win most all of the races aboard *Mermaid*.

Linton Rigg showed his concern for the future of the island by requesting from the English government a better water supply for the islanders, more reliable electricity, and an airport and a commercial dock to be built in Hillsborough. It was then he was awarded the title O.B.E (Officer of the British Empire) as a reward for his contribution to Carriacou and the Bahamas. Later he sold the Mermaid Tavern and retired permanently at his home at Tranquillity, where Bunny would visit him regularly along with other relatives.

In 1975 he became ill and traveled to Philadelphia for medical care, returning soon to Carriacou. During his last days his thoughts seemed to have been very much centered on his "mermaid." At age eighty-one his health deteriorated and in a little cemetery in Windward is the inscription, "Linton Rigg had hardly settled down in Carriacou before he started looking for something to do. One would have thought that for a man of his age (70), he would have had enough on his hands trying to run a hotel (Mermaid Tavern). But he was itching to do something which would popularize Carriacou for all times."

To The British Commissioner
Barbados
18 June, 1975

Sir:

    I would like to offer some help or assistance to Her Majesty's Government in the cost of supplying the island of Carriacou in the Grenadines with a new passenger pier suitable for the use of passenger vessels or small cruise ships. Such a pier would not only relieve the disastrous conditions now existing in that beautiful island, occupied by about eight thousand very humble and loyal people, but ensure some future prosperity to them.

    I am prepared to offer to her Majesty's Government any sum up to five hundred E.C. dollars to duplicate a subscription of the British Government to this project.

Yours Faithfully,
J. Linton Rigg

J. Linton Rigg
He died shortly after writing this letter. His commitment to the island and people is obvious. Hugh Cronyn wrote about Linton in his autobiography, *A Terrible Liar*, upon hiring him to contract a home being constructed in the Bahamas, "A telling description of Linton Rigg was provided in 1976, when he died and was buried ..."

photo overleaf:
Genesis launch in Windward, Carriacou

J. Linton Rigg, O.B.E.

Born in Jamaica in 1895, where his family have lived for generations … grandson of an Anglican bishop and son of a clergyman … educated as a naval architect … lived near Baltimore and for a while shifted from yachts to fox hunting. He married briefly and had a daughter he never saw.

Linton was a big man, quite deaf, very much self centered. He was an outspoken racist, but had devoted black friends, a practicing snob who simply excluded from his view people he thought below notice, and a pronounced male chauvinist. Because of his deafness, he spoke in a very loud voice. He was quarrelsome, a monoloquist, and an interrupter of other people's conversations, who bore no interruptions of his own.

Almost all the Bahamian islands in the 1940s were considered Cays – sandy, scrubby, and cut off from the wider world. All the details of the landscape are next to you, as you approach an anchorage or forge a trail. You don't fly through with speed, but slow down and cruise through. This is the place that attracted J. Linton Rigg after a career in the States as a yacht broker, designer, bon vivant, and person of questionable tastes who went cruising.

He came to explore, on his own boats, and wrote notes of the directions not for publication, because that's how a proper "English" yachtsman would have made his mark, but in his journals. It wasn't until 1949, when his *Bahama Islands* was published by Van Nostrand Sporting Books and got a substantial boost from the information that was anything but leftover from sailing and those who lured vessels upon the shore for salvage ("wracker tales"). Linton's hard work and hard fun and great effort would improve everyone's sailing experience in the Bahamas. So it didn't take much for him to get out and explore after World War I and things had settled a bit. He loved the islands. He wrote in his guide that a cruising ground for yachtsman,

photo opposite:
Linton receiving Order of British Empire medal

EPILOGUE :LINTON BIOGRAPHY

especially in winter months, would be hard to find as good as the Bahamas Islands anywhere in the world. He would leave us wonderful directions, as he says, "A man will find a cruising paradise of unbelievable charm and beauty, crystal clear water tinted by coral-pink sands, quite beautiful harbors abounding in maritime life: good sailing breezes at all times and probably the most perfect climate in the world." No doubt, these words demonstrate his affection for the Bahamas and also point to his decision to start the regatta and stay in the area as years passed.

More than sixty years later, the Family Island Regatta is famous as an international feature of the past and of the times ahead. Trouble is occasionally and rightly tagged to Linton as he did it his way, though he was recognized by the Brits as an honored statesman and awarded as such. But as we remember the early struggles for all good things – the American Revolution that so shaped the states, the islands colonization and battles for possession of these wonderful 1,000 islands that stretch 1,000 miles, battles that really only ended in the early 1970s with the Bahamas becoming a country – we know that without a man like Linton we would be poorer in many ways.

To be on an island surrounded by the seas or a boat underway was his supreme satisfaction. He lived a fascinating life that brought him towards a permanent mooring on Carriacou, Grenada. This was the most perfect island for him, to end his journey on the most beautiful place in the world.

Captain Joshua Slocum writes in his epic tale, that which can be described as the beginning of the pleasure cruising era, "My axe felled a stout oak tree near by for a keel, and Farmer Howard, for a small sum of money, hauled in this and enough timbers for the frame of the new vessel." That was in Boston in 1892.

On a June morning in 1898, Slocum arrived in Newport, Rhode Island, having sailed clear around the world, a voyage of 46,000 miles. J. Linton Rigg was born in Jamaica as Slocum was getting underway, an irony that is obvious in that Linton's life of sailing begins at the inception of pleasure cruising and leads to a lifetime of sailing benchmarks.

On May 5, 1494, Christopher Columbus, on his second voyage after a forty-eight-hour sail from Cuba, sees Jamaica rise – sheer and dark green – up from the sea, and his fleet makes landfall in St. Ann's Bay. Andres Bernaldez, a Spanish chaplain whom Columbus rested with after his voyage, deposited journals and described the voyage, communicating to us the admiral's enthusiasm for Jamaica: "It is the fairest island that eyes have beheld." He then goes on to say, "They have more canoes than elsewhere … and the natives are proud of possessing such fine ships."

J. Linton Rigg was a white Jamaican and well-known yachtsman in Corinthian circles. He had sailed with Carleton Mitchell on the last leg of the 1947 passage. Rigg published *Bahama Islands* (1949) two years later. It is similar in format to the Mitchell book and was for some years the standard yachting narrative for the Bahamas.

In 1960, at age sixty-five, he sold his house in George Town and bought a forty-three-foot wooden ketch, *Island Belle*. In it Rigg did a two-year trip from the Bahamas to Trinidad and back, the result of which was *The Alluring Antilles* (1963). Its chief claim is that, unlike Mitchell, Linton did not "race" through the islands; instead, he took his own sweet time, often staying in an anchorage for weeks, the better to know it. Unfortunately, Rigg had neither the intellect nor talent of Mitchell, and the book, despite its title, is a poor cousin to *Islands to Windward*. It is even a poor cousin to his own *Bahama Islands*. However, Rigg settled in the early 1960s in Carriacou, where he bought the Mermaid Tavern and started the Carriacou Regatta in 1965.

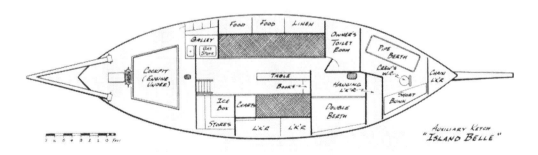

Plan of *Island Belle*, ketch. L.O.A. 43', L.W.L. 34' Beam 13', Draft 4'7" Headroom 6'6"

This was the first regatta in the Lesser Antilles. Two years later, in 1967, the Nicholson family started Antigua Race Week.

Of the original 1954 regatta in George Town, Rigg wrote in *Bahama Islands* (third edition, 1959): "It all started when the late Ward Wheelock visited me in my home at George Town in 1953. Mr. Wheelock, having made a great deal of money in the advertising business in Philadelphia, decided to spend the rest of his life working for the improvement of understanding and relationship between the peoples of the world. He had the very strongest conviction that therein lay the only solution to the end of wars. We discussed the various means of getting people of different races and nationalities to meet each other, and agreed that only when they met together to have fun were the results always happy. As my own consuming interest has always been in sailing boats, their design, construction, and the preservation of existing sailing fleets, we had a meeting of minds, and decided that a regatta for the working boats of the islands would go a long way to accomplish what we both desired."

By the time Rigg died on the island in 1976, boat building was revived and a new generation of builders had learned the traditional skills. Yachting, like so much else, became a corporate enterprise marked by aggressive marketing. Indeed, the Lesser Antilles today are less an archipelago than a marketplace. Or are they merely but a click in cyberspace? It was yachtsmen, in any case, who spearheaded the rediscovery of the islands, which the end of slavery in 1834 had left in economic ruin, political neglect, and social dismay for more than a century. Carleton Mitchell's remarkable cruise in 1947 signaled at once an awakening of yachtsmen to the islands and the islands' awakening to the modern world. Can you imagine being a lone yachtsman surrounded by engineless sloops and schooners in St. George's Harbor or Admiralty Bay

Linton on *Island Belle*

or English Harbour? Never again will yachtsmen encounter the unspoiled places that seemed, for them if not the inhabitants, a paradise on earth. The early yachtsmen may have been lucky to experience such "unspoiled beauty," but the peoples of the Lesser Antilles were equally lucky that the yachtsmen came along and brought tourism with them.

Linton wearing his OBE medal

The Filatonga Picture

When *Filatonga* was finally completed and commissioned I asked my very good friend Charles Patterson, the now famous marine painter, to come and spend a weekend with me on her. He and I both Englishmen, had come to New York to make our living, and neither of us had much money to go along. After that weekend he said, "I also as you did, fell in love with her and someday would like to paint her."

About one year later he phoned me and asked me to see his favorite picture of a yacht racing at sea. When I went to his studio and saw it tears came to my eyes. He said, "I did it for you, and it's what I call my Cinderella picture, and reminds me of Shaw's Pygmailion, now I want you to help me with some of the details: the rigging, the proper sails, and of course the flags."

When it had all been completed many yachtsmen came to see it, including Harold Vanderbuilt, who wished to buy it. Patterson said, " Mr. Vanderbuilt no one can buy this, and I'm giving to my old friend Linton Rigg and it will always be his as long as he likes as he has promised me that he'll never sell it. I admire Linton Rigg for what he has done for taking this lovely girl out of her unfortunate life of sin and making her a true lady again."

Mr. Vanderbuilt subsequently gave Charles Patterson the commission to paint pictures of two of his favorite yachts and paid Patterson a princely sum for them.

I never gave it away or sold it to anyone. However when I had sold my house in Annapolis and my brother Bunny had built himself a new house, "Replica", I loaned the painting to him with the understanding that he could have it in his house as long as he wanted to have it hanging there. J.L.R.

This is as written in Linton's logbook along with his will and other notes.

THE FILATONGA PICTURE

"To desire nothing beyond what you have is surely happiness. Aboard a boat it is frequently possible to achieve just that: that is why sailing is a way of life, one of the finest of lives."
The Winds Call by Carleton Mitchell

photo opposite:
Last photo of J. Linton Rigg, at *Tranquillity*, his home in Windward, Carriacou

A United States Coast Guard licensed captain, Capt. Art Ross has credentials, sailing experience, and blue water knowledge combined with a passion for the sea and boats. Those that know or sail with him find that this love of the water and related topics is infectious, interesting, and always fun. He has owned and built both wood and fiberglass boats, has delivered charter boats to the Caribbean from the States, teaches sailing, and works as a charter captain for a Chesapeake Bay charter business. Along the way, Capt. Art has raced from Virginia to the Virgin Islands, captaining a forty-seven-foot sailboat; he delivered the *Mimi*, an eighty-foot wooden teaching schooner, from Baltimore to Philadelphia in a late season snow squall. He captained the *Half Moon*, a New York City dinner cruise boat that would visit the Statue of Liberty and the aircraft carrier *Intrepid* at night with 350 passengers aboard.

Yellowbird after the Carriacou Regatta, 2004

He resides in New Hope, Pennsylvania, where he teaches introduction to sailing at a local community college, but spends most of his time aboard his forty-four-year-old sailboat in the Chesapeake Bay and works occasionally as a charter captain. He sails with, and is a member of, the prestigious Ocean Cruising Club, London, England, recently sailing in their club rally celebrating its fiftieth anniversary with a cruise of the Gulf Islands, Vancouver, British Columbia. He is also a current member of the Chesapeake Area Professional Captains Association, and recently a member of the USCG Auxiliary.

Art had an opportunity to crew on *Yellowbird*, when it was the winner of the 2004 Carriacou Regatta, a coincidence that he finds at this juncture a favorite memory as well.

Art's passion for sailing is only surpassed by his wish to have all those he meets join him aboard on a breezy day to share those wonderful experiences together.

Rail meat on *Yellowbird*, 2004

ART ROSS: AUTHOR BIOGRAPHY

22784090R00076

Made in the USA
San Bernardino, CA
21 July 2015